Conducting Applied Psychological Research

Conducting Applied Psychological Research: A Practical Guide

Charlotte Wilson

 Open University Press

Open University Press
McGraw Hill
Unit 4
Foundation Park
Roxborough Way
Maidenhead
SL6 3UD

email: emea_uk_ireland@mheducation.com
world wide web: www.mheducation.co.uk

Commissioning Editor: Beth Summers
Editorial Assistant: Hannah Jones
Content Product Manager: Graham Jones

A catalogue record of this book is available from the British Library

ISBN-13: 978-0-3352-5009-7
ISBN-10: 0335250092
eISBN: 978-0-3352-5010-3

Library of Congress Cataloging-in-Publication Data
CIP data applied for

Typeset by Transforma Pvt. Ltd., Chennai, India

Praise page

"This book is aimed at those new to research or who might be feeling nervous about undertaking a new project. I like that it takes a pragmatic approach to introducing a range of methods, including covering different types of review. It describes how to avoid common pitfalls. It is most likely to be helpful in the process of deciding on the type of approach to take for a project. Further reading will be necessary to ensure that readers use sufficiently sophisticated analysis to enable their work to reach publishable standard, and this book has helpful signposting to other appropriate sources."

Professor Andrew R Thompson,
Programme Director of the South Wales
Clinical Psychology Training Programme

"This is such a useful book for applied psychology researchers - everything you need to think about at the start of a new study is there in one place. I can see me recommending this to all of my students, but also as a quick way of checking I've covered all bases when I'm planning a new project myself."

Sam Cartwright-Hatton,
Professor of Clinical Child Psychology,
University of Sussex, UK

Contents

List of Boxes

List of Figures and Tables

Figures

Table

Acknowledgements

I owe a huge debt of gratitude to Hannah Jones, Graham Jones and the team at McGraw-Hill for their guidance, support and patience in the writing and production of this book. Without this I would never have got it over the line. The book itself would not have been possible without all the wonderful students and colleagues I have worked with over the years. I have learned so much from them and by working with them. It has truly been a privilege to be part of so many research journeys, and through that to be a part of so many participant's experiences. It also would not have been possible without my family. Thanks to Katherine and Lizzy for asking difficult questions that make me think about how you answer difficult questions in reasonable ways. Thanks to Paul for conversations about what is science and what good research looks like. Thanks to Hazel for making me question who is being included and who we are not noticing or paying attention to. And most of all, thanks to George for always trying to answer even my most difficult or unusual questions and for encouraging me to ask and to answer questions. This book is dedicated to him.

Prologue

Welcome! I'm delighted you have picked up this book and I hope that it helps you with your aim of undertaking applied psychological research. It is aimed at anyone who wants to do research, but isn't sure exactly where to start. That might be because you haven't done research before, or because you haven't done research for a while, or because you think it may need a different research approach to the one you usually take. I hope this book helps you work out the best way of answering your research question and gives you some tips for what to do and what to avoid.

It took me a long time to work out that applied psychological research might look different from more fundamental psychological research, and this book charts part of that journey to understanding why we do research and what kinds of knowledge we produce when we do. I am not a focused researcher – there isn't one particular topic or one particular approach that I take. I put this down to wanting to understand things as they really are, and that people and systems – the focus of applied psychological research – are very complicated! People don't operate in a vacuum; they are impacted by the people around them, their wider social worlds, their physical environment, their political environment, and by their experiences. As a practitioner it is my job to understand how people work in general, but to apply this knowledge to the specific individual in front of me. This merging of the general theories, empirical findings, with the individuality of each person means that some of the fundamental psychological research that has been done doesn't relate to my professional work. People are messy – our lives are messy and therefore the principles and theories that help us understand each other are likely to be messy. My research has been focused on capturing enough of this mess while keeping the research methods as valid as possible.

There are three sections to this book. The first highlights common features of applied psychological research – the question, the participants and philosophy and theory. These chapters are relevant to anyone doing applied psychological research. The next 12 chapters each outline a different research approach. These include key approaches that can be helpful in understanding people in real life. They include different quantitative, qualitative and mixed methods approaches. You may already have an idea about what approach you want to take, or you might be deciding between two or three different approaches. Either way, each of these chapters stands alone and can be read when needed. The final section is about dissemination of your research. Academics have standard ways of disseminating their work, and these are included in this section, but as an applied researcher, there might be alternative or additional ways of disseminating your research when it is completed. This chapter works through how to decide how to disseminate and how to ensure you are communicating with your audience.

A word of warning: I am a clinical psychologist by training and my clinical work tends to be with children and families. This clearly impacts how I think about research and will impact my examples throughout the group. I have tried to include a variety of examples from developmental, clinical and health psychology, and where possible, occupational and organisational psychology, but these are inevitably based on my own experience. I am also passionate about inclusion and diversity and you will see these themes come through many of the chapters. It is not something we often foreground in research textbooks, so I hope that my discussion prompts you to think about these issues and how they are relevant in your research.

My wish is that you find the book useful, and that it makes you think 'I can do this. I can do research.' Good quality applied research is so valuable for everyone who ever needed a service, or support, or to be understood, and the best people to do that research are those people who are embedded in those services, whether as practitioners or in training.

Best of luck!

1 Questions are messy

How often have you read in a paper that this research should be done because it has not been done before? Sometimes when you read the research you know why! There are some questions that don't need answering. Conversely, there is a lot of research out there and sometimes a question very close to the question you are asking has already been answered. This chapter aims to walk you through how to translate a research topic or interest into a research question. The chapters that follow can help you determine what research methods can help you answer that question. In reality, these aspects of your research are interlinked and impact each other, but the best place to start is with your question.

In general, there appear to be two main ways in which research questions arise. Sometimes there is existing research, maybe an existing model or framework that needs testing, and there is an obvious next step. There may be a specific gap in the literature that needs filling. In this case the researcher has probably spent a good amount of time looking at the research that has already been done, identified what else needs to be known and has identified a research question that fills in that gap. The problem with this in applied research is that it might be that the research question is not the right one. It might be that filling the gap is not particularly important to the people you work with, or it might be that the whole topic is not the right one. The other approach to developing a research question is when you have observed something interesting about the world around you. It might be in your clinic or your classroom, it might be in your community or a community you have visited or heard about. The problem with this approach is that often there is similar research that has already been done, or that there is a good reason why the research has not been done. In applied research we run the risk of ploughing ahead with our ideas without fully exploring what has been done and thus waste both our own time and that of our participants. So what can we do about this?

Starting point one: Going from observation to question

You have observed something you are curious about. Maybe the child in your class who always fiddles with her pencil seems to work better when there is a fair bit of noise in the classroom. Maybe the people in your clinic with families who bring them to appointments seem to be doing better than the ones that come alone. Maybe you've noticed that your colleagues are more sympathetic towards patients who are grateful and therefore that they tend to get a better service. Sometimes you might want to pursue some of these ideas by doing research. That might be because of your own curiosity, or because you want to test your ideas, or because you want others to acknowledge your observations. Noticing that things could be better for marginalised, sick, or vulnerable people or that we could keep more people safe and happy in general is a valuable driver of a lot of excellent applied research. You might be great at managing the noise level in your classroom to ensure that all students can learn, but you might be working in an environment where other teachers believe it must be silent for all children to learn, or conversely that the noise level doesn't matter at all. You might give equal time to the people who come to clinic with and without their families, but you might wonder about whether the clinic can do something to promote social support for all.

So, you've made an observation, you are interested in testing it, so how do you start? The first thing to do is to identify a possible *research* question. A good research question should be:

Answerable. You should be able to answer the question. Some questions just cannot be answered using a scientific method, including questions about the past or uncovering certain aspects of the unconscious mind, and some questions should not be asked ethically. You need to think about whether the question you are asking is something that reasonably can be answered using standard research methods.

Aligned with the method used to test it. Lots of questions can be answered using a variety of methods, but some methods are better than others at answering particular questions. If you are interested in experiences, you probably want to think about qualitative methods, and if you want to test the difference between two groups, you want to think about quantitative methods. A good research question is well aligned with the methods used to answer it.

A 'goldilocks' size. A good research question is just the right size. You probably aren't going to be able to eliminate malaria (unless you have the fortune of Bill Gates to employ teams of researchers), but you also cannot learn very much by giving questionnaires to three people. The available sample size should not limit the questions you can ask, but it might help you think about the scope of the research question.

Interesting and important to someone other than you. Some of us have minds that constantly throw up interesting questions about the world. Some of us have children, friends or family that do this for us! But these questions don't all need answering. If you are using public funds, either directly through research funding, or through your own time if that is publicly funded, and if you are using the time and emotional work of your participants, then it is important to ask important questions.

Not already answered. This last point is where to start if you have an observation. With your observation you have identified a provisional question or area of interest. The first question is to ask yourself: has someone else noticed this and have they done any research into the topic? Google Scholar is your friend in this. Google Scholar organises its responses by relevance. That means that the things most relevant to your question should come up first. The way it works also means you can type your whole question into a single search box to see what comes up. If there is nothing there then it doesn't mean that nothing exists, but it is a clear indication that the field isn't swimming in research studies! Searching for existing literature is a skill in itself and is reviewed more thoroughly in Chapter 4 about systematic reviewing. Here, let's think about how to expand your search in order to look for relevant research that has already been done.

Step one: Put your entire research question/observation into Google Scholar with the additional words review, meta-analysis, and/or meta-synthesis. This will give you any reviews of the topic. Reviews are great places to start. If there aren't any reviews (see also step four) then you will have to try and find individual papers.

Step two: Throw your entire research question into Google Scholar without the words review, meta-analysis, or meta-synthesis. Scroll through the first few pages of responses to see what has been done in the area.

Step three: Think about alternatives to some of your key words. If you are interested in mental health in a prison population, for example, you could search for recidivism, offending, maybe even crime and wellbeing. If you are interested in social support, you could search for friendship, connection, community. If you can't think of any synonyms, try a synonym finder.

Step four: Check to see if there are particular places or journals that the interesting research has been published. Many academic journals have searchable contents lists. Check out the key journals in the topic for more research. If your discipline has a review journal (for example, *Clinical Psychology Review*) specifically check that out to see if there is a review in a directly relevant or closely relevant topic.

Step five: With your favourite finds from the above steps check out the reference lists for additional papers to read, and also check out what papers have cited them – this can be done in Google Scholar, in many of the more formal search engines and sometimes in the journal website (when the journal is part of a larger organisation such as Sage, Springer or Wiley).

At this stage you are scoping out what has already been done to determine whether you need to do your study at all. If your study is high stakes and you need to make sure you are not going to be pipped at the post by other researchers, then also check out the databases of registered studies. Not being in one of these databases is no guarantee that the study isn't being done somewhere, but it is always worth checking.

When you have a good number of papers, find a quiet place, grab a coffee, and read. If your professional life is busy then this can be hard to prioritise, but it is crucial. Not only can it save you time if the study has already been done, but it can also highlight some of the difficulties in your research topic. Do you notice that in all the studies 100 people are approached but only 10 take part? That suggests that recruitment is going to be hard. Do you notice that each study uses different questionnaires that they made up themselves? That suggests that there aren't good measures for the variable you are interested in. Also, it might be that a recent paper, or, even better, a recent review, highlights key things that need doing next in the field and you can use some of their ideas to determine your research question. While you are reading it is worth starting to take notes on what research has been done, which participants have been involved, what the findings are, and what the researchers recommend as next steps in research. As you continue reading you may find yourself wanting to note more details about particular aspects of the research, such as the measures used, or the analysis strategy employed, but initial notes can be quite simple. You are trying to determine how much your research question can be answered using the existing research (see also Chapter 4 about doing this systematically), while also starting to think about what kinds of methods might be suitable to answer your particular question.

What if there really hasn't been any research done on your topic?

Sometimes there will be very few, or no papers on your topic. Now you need to think more broadly about what literature is relevant. It is likely that there is literature on one aspect of your research, such as the participants, or the psychological construct, but not the combination of the two. Your reading therefore will likely start with the more general literature on the participants or the construct. Look out for models or frameworks in the wider literature that might be relevant to your question, and try and look for research that tests the model in a similar participant group. Using these models and frameworks you can try to see what research has already been done on the different aspects of the model and what the gaps are. The aim here is not to work out what gap to fill, but to determine how much your research question has already been answered and what else you want to know about your observation.

If you are still stuck, then you might want to ask why. If no-one has ever done any research like yours is anyone else interested in your research topic? Who will your research benefit? There is a place for completely new ground-breaking research, but if there are public funds funding the research, then maybe it is worth thinking carefully about whether your participants will benefit from your research.

By starting with reading, you will also be starting to think about the other points above – answerable, interesting questions that are the right size for your time and resources, and that can be answered using standard research methods. I have had colleagues and students come to me with interesting questions that just can't be answered in a single research study. I have had colleagues and students come to with me a question that is interesting for the service, but that does not add to our research literature overall as the scope is small and replicates a well-known finding. Both kinds of questions can be shaped into a suitable research project, but they take a little more work before they are good research questions.

Starting point two: I have to do a research project, what do I do?

Hopefully there are things you are interested in and you may even have started to develop possible ideas or questions. But sometimes if you have to do research then the process is somewhat different. If you have an open choice of project, spend some time thinking about things that have got you curious or angry or confused. An emotional reaction to something or someone can highlight something that we may want to know more about. Sometimes this process is best done with a colleague or friend, or potential supervisor, who can ask questions to help you explore what it is that interests you. If this is your route, then as soon as you have your topic or general area, you can start at the beginning of the last section and go from observation to question.

If you do not have a free choice – there are often several supervisors offering projects – then it is still worth thinking about which to choose. There are three key things to think about: the supervisor, the methodology, and topic. In my experience, most people choose a research project based on the last of these; they are interested in children's development, or autism, or diabetes, or perception, or psychotherapy, and they choose a supervisor with expertise in the topic. This is not a bad place to start, but I urge you to consider the other two aspects of the experience too. The methods you are going to use to answer your research question can have a huge impact on the experience of doing the research. Are you going to get to meet with your participants or is it all remote? And which would you prefer? Are you going to have to manage lots of different sources of recruitment and lots of different gatekeepers in order to get a large sample size, or are you going to be in control of (and therefore fully responsible for) recruitment yourself? Is the project quantitative (lots of work up front ensuring that you have the measures and procedures correct for the question, no need to spend too much time thinking of your own role in the research) or qualitative (lots of work down the line, possibly when you have exams, as you struggle with the uncertainties of analysis, necessity for reflexivity and understanding your own research philosophy and own positionality), or mixed methods (best and worst of both worlds!)? Finally, what about the supervisor? Don't believe all rumours, but talking to people who have been supervised by the supervisor previously will tell you whether they are hands on (high levels of support, but with the risk of micro-managing every aspect of the project), or hands off (no support or guidance, but no interference). They might be able to tell you whether they are glass-half-full people (everything is great, it just needs a complete re-write) or glass-half-empty people (it is dreadful, there is so much work to do, you need to re-think this one sentence). At the very bad end, some supervisors are bullies or are not available for any supervision, but most supervisors are just human. They have developed their own strengths and weaknesses in supervisory practice, and if you have a choice, it is best to choose someone who will complement your own skills. Are you good at working independently? You will be fine with a hands-off supervisor. Do you have good knowledge of the topic, but are scared about the research process? You need someone who feels it is their job to walk you through the process and support you in your decisions. Are you wanting to do qualitative research in a topic that has personal importance to you? You need a supervisor who you can trust, even with your personal views and values. Play to your strengths and balance the different aspects of the research to your benefit.

If you are choosing a project from a selection of projects then it is less likely that you will have to start from scratch with the reading as your supervisor will be able to guide you as to what to read to understand the topic, but you might want to add to this using the steps above. If not, then you can start at the next step.

Going from reading to planning

So, you have identified your interest and your topic, you have searched the literature for studies that can help you answer this and you have hopefully identified something that you could do to add to the literature, satisfy your own curiosity, and make things better for your participants. How do you go from this to determining your question and your method?

Start by writing down what you want to find out. Your aim here is to become aware of your own research agenda. We'll talk more about reflexivity in the chapters on qualitative research, but it is important in all applied research. If we expect to find something specific, then we might be tempted to plan a study that finds just this. Take the example above about the child who focuses more when there is noise in the classroom. It is clear that we want to find that a noisy classroom is better for some children, because that is what we have experienced. However, what might we not pay attention to in thinking like this? We might not pay attention to other children who find a noisy classroom more difficult to concentrate in, we might not pay attention to other situations in which these children concentrate well, and we might not pay attention to the age of the child and how this interacts with whether they concentrate better or worse in this noisy environment. So, when I say write down what you want to find, interrogate your answer a little more. Are you interested in the best conditions for learning for these kinds of children? Are you interested in the best classroom environment for the whole class, or are you interested in a more fundamental question about which learning processes (meta-cognition, attention switching, planning) are affected by a noisy environment? Maybe you are simply interested in what is going on for the particular child in your classroom and what their experience is of learning. From this one observation comes lots of different questions. You can read other examples of going from observation to question in each of the chapters, but there are a few examples to get you started in Box 1.1.

From your list of possible questions, you are now ready to think about methods. You might have a good idea about methods from your own training and experience. You might have read some good studies with methods that you could borrow. You might have a study from a different topic that has stayed with you because the method was different and exciting (mostly these are cool experiments), or that has stayed with you because the results were really meaningful and made you think about how you could improve your practice (often these are qualitative). If the method isn't obvious from the question, then have a look through the following chapters to see if there is a method that can help you answer the question.

This process is often far from linear. You start with a clear idea of who your participants are, but then the literature tells you that the question has already been answered. You start with a clear question, but then realise that it is a lifetime's work, not a single study. You have read a brilliant study and want to use the methodology but realise that you can't manipulate the variable you are interested in in the same way. If this book is helpful to you, you will go back and forth between this chapter, the next chapter on participants and then some of the different chapters on specific methodologies. Over several iterations, your research question will come together with your methodology and your study will be on its way.

Box 1.1: One problem, lots of solutions

In applied psychological research there are lots of different ways of answering one question. Here is an example:

The observation/problem:
In my clinical work I noticed that although I had learned all about the kinds of thoughts adults had when they were having a panic attack, the adolescents I was seeing who were experiencing panic attacks did not seem to have the same kinds of thoughts.

How could I investigate this?
I could:

Look into existing research. I could try and do a review of studies that explore the kinds of thoughts adolescents have during a panic attack.

Search for existing data sets on adolescent panic that I might be able to extract data from on the content of thoughts for secondary analysis. I wouldn't expect to find many datasets like this but someone who has run a therapy trial for adolescents with panic disorder might have this kind of data, or if there is a local Cognitive Behavioural Therapy clinic, they might routinely collect this data.

Design a between-groups study. I could recruit both adolescents and adults who have panic attacks and ask them about their thoughts during a panic attack and then look at the differences.

Test the well-validated cognitive model of panic in adolescents. I could see if the thoughts adolescents have increase the feelings of anxiety, and if this leads to an upwards spiral culminating in a panic attack. This could be done in a cross-sectional study by testing the links between different factors statistically, or I could try and manipulate one aspect of the process to see if it has an impact on a different part of the process in an experimental design.

Survey adolescents about their thoughts when they are feeling panicky. I could then classify them into useful categories such as thoughts about death, thoughts about losing control, or thoughts about endlessness.

Use a sequential mixed methods approach. I could start by asking a few adolescents about their experiences of panic attacks and use this to develop a model, and then collect further data from adolescents who have different experiences of panic to test this model.

Do in-depth interviews with a small number of adolescents who experience panic. I could try and get at the core of what a panic attack is experientially.

Interview some adolescents about their experiences of panic using a cognitive-behavioural framework. I could try and find out their thoughts, feelings and behaviours before, during, and after a panic attack, and find meaningful conceptual themes that illustrate the experience.

How do I choose which one?

In order to determine which question I am going to ask and therefore which approach to take I am going to ask myself:

What do I really want to know? For example, I only want to know whether there are differences between adults and adolescents because I think it might impact on what I need to do to help. Therefore, it might be more interesting to look at the model of panic and whether it works for adolescents than it would to simply compare adults and adolescents.

Are there any restrictions to what participants I might be able to recruit and support? If I'm working in an adolescent service I might find it hard to recruit an adult sample and therefore I might rule out a between groups approach. If I'm an undergraduate I might not feel I have the skills to support adolescents to talk in depth about their experiences of panic so I might rule out a qualitative interview approach. I might feel, maybe due to personal experience, that panic is such a difficult experience I want to see what a non-anxious set of adolescents do and so I might choose an experimental design where we can test a hypothesis without further distressing adolescents experiencing panic attacks.

What are my research strengths or needs? If you are starting out in research you might want to think about whether you naturally gravitate towards quantitative research or qualitative research in your thinking. You might think about whether you are an organised person who will be able to keep in touch with lots of different services to ensure they are giving out information sheets to recruit a large sample. You might think about how the project fits into your life – quantitative research needs of a lot of work up front – you need to really have a good question, a good design and good measures, and then a large sample. Qualitative research needs a lot of work when you have the data as the analysis is taxing, both intellectually and emotionally (depending on the topic) and you have to be able to sit with uncertainty.

What context am I doing this research in? or *What am I doing this research for?* If you are part of an academic research department things like journal impact factors, research funding, etc. might be important. If you are in a hospital setting, doing something that might persuade your colleagues or commissioners might be more important to you.

2 Participants

One of the things that makes applied research both rewarding and tricky is the participants. Rarely do we want to recruit undergraduate psychology students to answer our questions, instead we want to work with the very people who are impacted by the phenomena we are interested in. This comes with its own challenges, but most of these are manageable, and the relevance of the data we collect makes it worthwhile!

Deciding on participant characteristics

In Chapter 1 we explored how to develop our research questions and make our messy practical questions into ones we can answer using research. Although we are thinking about our participants in this chapter, the two things go together, and we need to think about our participants in conjunction with thinking about our question. These two things go together with our methodology, so when you are choosing who you want your participants to be, you need to be thinking of the question and the method.

Sometimes we want to understand the experience of people who have a certain condition, or who have experienced a certain life event. For example, you might want to know about children who struggle with reading and writing or have a diagnosis of dyslexia. You might want to know about people who have experienced a heart attack. You might want to know about people who fly planes regularly. If you want to hear from the people directly then you have no choice about your participants. You still have to think about inclusion and exclusion criteria, and you still have to deal with gatekeepers (see below), but it is clear who your potential participants are.

However, sometimes you might be interested in a process or something that occurs along a continuum, such as whether reading ability is related to meta-cognition, or whether appraisals of negative mood are associated with persistence of such moods. It might be easier to test this process in an analogue sample, and indeed this might be more ethical as well (see discussion of ethics in Chapter 6).

Inclusion and exclusion criteria

Once you have an idea of the kind of participants you would like to include in your research, the next step is to decide your inclusion and exclusion criteria. The things below could be part of your decisions.

Age of participants. You might want to limit the age of your participants because you are interested in a particular developmental period, such as infancy or older adulthood. You might want a homogenous sample of people and therefore want them to be of a similar age. It might also be that diagnostic criteria, innovations in treatment, or policy changed at some point and so you want to include people who got their diagnosis before (or after) the change or include people who have benefited (or haven't) from changes in treatment. You might only be interested in digital natives who grew up with and use modern technology, or digital immigrants who have had to learn how to use it. However, many people choose an age range because they have seen it done in papers. I would ask yourself, is there a genuine reason for excluding certain participants because of their age? Are we excluding certain people from research and are we reducing the generalisability of our research by restricting an age range? In applied research we are often balancing internal validity with external validity (see Box 2.1). Some researchers will always aim to maximise internal validity by ensuring that their participants are as similar as possible, however, in applied research we may want to maximise our external validity to ensure that our findings have applicability across a wide range of people.

Box 2.1: Validity

Validity is important in all research, and especially in quantitative research. In experiments we want to know that the dependent variable changed as a result of manipulating the independent variable and not because of something else. However, we also want to know whether our result is applicable to people who weren't involved in our experiment. In other quantitative studies we want to know that our measures measure the construct they are designed to and that they do this reliably (emphasising statistical invariance in the structure, internal consistency, and stability), but we also want to know that they are measuring something that is important to measure in a way that represents how the construct works in the real world. These are two different kinds of validity and often research must balance them.

Figure 2.1 Balancing internal and external validity in applied psychological research

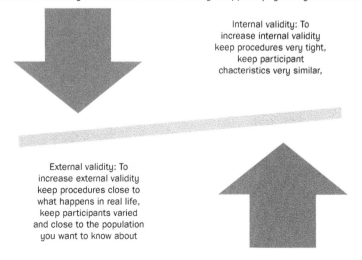

Internal validity: To increase internal validity keep procedures very tight, keep participant chacteristics very similar,

External validity: To increase external validity keep procedures close to what happens in real life, keep participants varied and close to the population you want to know about

Language use/primary language. Many applied researchers working in English-speaking countries have inclusion criteria about English language competence. This might be important for the validity of measures – many measures do not have validated translations, and so the validity of using adapted versions is questionable. It might be important for the validity of the analysis strategy; if you are qualitatively analysing language use, then the translation of other languages into your own language might miss some of the nuances or meaning inherent in the words spoken. Beyond this, once again we must question whether it is absolutely necessary for answering our research question to restrict the language of our participants. Certainly, there has been a shift from including participants who have English as a first language, to including participants who have sufficient English to answer our questions. Some participants might need support with their language (see also below on capacity to consent), but our research should be designed to support that. Often, applied research is done by students and by the professionals working in the field, and therefore it is often done on a restricted budget, but perhaps inclusion should be prioritised in research in the same way they are in the services we work in.

Diagnostic status. In the field of health, whether physical or mental health, we often want to recruit people with specific diagnoses. This seems quite simple, but it can be more complicated. One complication is additional diagnoses or co-morbidity. Excluding people with additional diagnoses may be done to maximise internal validity, for example, treating people with health anxiety may be impacted by including those with medical health conditions, so you may start by excluding them. It may also be done to reduce risk. Quite often if someone is at very high risk, for example, they are very sick, or they are at risk of harming themselves, they are excluded because the researchers are not well placed to manage this risk and it is important not to put people at additional risk. When we, or someone in the research team, is working in the service directly it might be possible to manage this risk within the service in addition to running the research project. It might also be more important to maximise external validity of the treatment in order to be able to offer it to anyone in the service. Once again, applied research might take a different approach to mainstream research.

You might want to think about who has to have made the diagnosis. It might be important that the research team do this themselves to ensure that the right diagnoses have been made and to ensure you have a good understanding of additional relevant diagnoses. However, this often takes a lot of time and training, and you might not have the resources to do this. You might also want to consider the impact that going through detailed diagnostic questions may have on the participant. They may feel not believed, or conversely, they may not accept the diagnosis and feel threatened by the process. It might be tiring to repeatedly go through similar questions, and it might be contradictory to the purpose and aims of the research, for example, if you are prioritising the lived experience of the person and taking a constructionist approach, then the positivist/empiricist approach to diagnosis might conflict with this. There might be some conditions where the diagnosis is extremely stigmatising, and people will not want to take part if you advertise the study to be about that. There might be some diagnoses that are difficult to get due to service limitations and therefore it is common for people to self-diagnose.

Even if your participants have a particular diagnosis you might want to think about whether there are subgroups that you want to include in the research. This translates into whether there are subgroups that you need in order to answer your research question. You may need people who have a particular severity of their disorder or condition, or consider whether you need them to have recovered for a certain amount of time, or whether they need to have had their diagnosis for a certain amount of time. Again, asking these questions can be sensitive and it might be that they need to be part of the gatekeeping process rather than something that is done in the research process (see below).

Capacity to consent. In most of our research we require our participants to consent to take part. In the past some people were considered not to have this ability, such as people with intellectual disabilities or people with severe mental illness. However, in many countries this has been challenged, and more recently consent and the capacity to consent has been viewed as a process and therefore there are no automatic situations in which someone cannot consent. Biros (2018) provides a good outline of the issues involved in informed consent and assessing someone's capacity to consent. If you are embedded in a service then you may be familiar with getting consent from people who require support in giving it, but if not, you may want to consider working closely with people who do work in the service to help you work out how to do this. This process may take more time and more skills, but the benefits of including people who aren't usually included in research outweigh these challenges.

Inclusion/exclusion criteria specific to different methods. Your research design might also influence the inclusion and exclusion criteria more specifically. For example, if you are doing an IPA study (see Chapter 14), then you will be looking for a homogenous sample of participants. That means they must share key characteristics. By contrast, if you are doing a grounded theory study (Chapter 13) you will be looking for people who are varied and who have varied experiences. If you want to compare two groups, a clinical group and a control group, you might want your control group *not* to have any features of the clinical disorder or condition. You might also want to match them on age, cognitive ability, gender, SES, ethnicity, etc. in order to ensure that the changes are due to the main condition of interest rather than any of these other characteristics.

Sample size: How many is enough?

There are a lot of different methods that you can use to answer research questions with relatively small sample sizes. Sometimes there is an assumption that having a small sample size means you have to do qualitative research (or vice versa: qualitative research means small sample sizes), but other designs can be used with small numbers of participants, from recruiting no participants yourself (see Chapters 4 and 5 on using existing datasets and synthesising literature) to designing your question and method so that it can be answered with relatively few participants.

The over-arching principle in determining your sample size is how many participants you need to answer your research question appropriately. When you are analysing your data statistically, then this is determined by your predicted effect size and your required power as well as by the test you are using. In general, the more variables you want to put into your analysis – either because it is important in your question, or because you need to control for important but extraneous variables – the larger the sample size you need. The smaller the effect you are likely to see, the larger the number of participants you need. Finally, the greater the power you wish your study to have, the larger the number of participants you will need. There are a few ways of calculating your sample size. In the literature you will find lots of rules of thumb, but that's just what they are – rules of thumb. You risk type two error and not rejecting the null hypothesis when you should. Luckily there are lots of books, papers and even calculators to help you determine your sample size. You need to know your analysis strategy before you calculate your sample size, but that is also good science. Check out Bhandari's article that outlines these key features of quantitative research.

Quantitative research: Sample size calculators

Note: The website addresses provided below are subject to change. You can always do an internet search for 'online power calculator' or 'online sample size calculator' if these aren't current.

When you know how highly powered you want your study to be, what you want to set your significance level at, what analyses you are going to do, and what effect size you think is important for your study, then it is possible to calculate what sample size you need. You can do this by hand, but it is more common to use a specific calculator.

Survey Monkey and Qualtrics both have their own sample size calculators, so you can use the same software to calculate your sample size as you do to distribute your measures.

GPower is a free computer programme that you can download: https://www.psychologie.hhu.de/arbeitsgruppen/allgemeine-psychologie-und-arbeitspsychologie/gpower

It is a powerful sample size/power calculator that has lots of different options for statistical analyses. It can take a short while to find your way around because of this, but it does mean that once you know how to use it you won't need another sample size calculator.

ClinCalc has a somewhat more straightforward interface and is great if you are looking at a relatively simple design such as a between groups design. https://clincalc.com/stats/samplesize.aspx

PowerandSampleSize.com is another website that doesn't require any downloads (unlike GPower) but has a lot of different calculators depending on what study design/analysis you are using (unlike ClinCalc). One of the lovely aspects of this site is that you get a graph to explore to determine what happens when you change your parameters, which means you don't have to repeatedly check what happens if you change your proposed alpha or beta value. http://powerandsamplesize.com/Calculators/

Qualitative research: Knowing your methodology

If you are doing qualitative research, then the same overarching principle is helpful in determining your sample size: how many participants do you need to answer your research question appropriately? Your research aim should align with the quality and quantity of data you analyse, and the quality and quantity of data is partially determined by how many participants you interview. Each individual approach has differing guidance on how many participants are needed. In IPA a small number of similar/homogenous participants that can give a rich account of the phenomenon of interest is recommended. In grounded theory a larger number of varying participants is required to develop a theory. Reflexive thematic analysis is flexible with respect to numbers of participants, but given the focus is understanding meaning and context, then you need sufficient participants to explore this fully. Many qualitative studies and checklists for quality in qualitative research discuss saturation as an aim and as a guide for determining the number of participants, but in the history of the different methods, only grounded theory really endorses it. Indeed, only one type of grounded theory endorses it. Braun and Clarke write convincingly about why it isn't a useful aim in qualitative research (see Chapter 12). Some of this comes down to the difference between the epistemology of saturation and the epistemology of much of qualitative research.

Recruitment strategies and gatekeepers

One of the most stressful aspects of research is recruitment. Whether you are looking for a small number of very similar participants or whether you are trying to recruit a large number of participants with a particular condition or diagnosis, you will work hard to get your participants. Each recruitment method has its benefits and drawbacks, and if you have a choice, it may be worth considering what your own strengths are and then to play to your strengths.

Open recruitment: Using media, social media, word of mouth, participant panels and professional participant recruitment

For some studies you can throw your net wide and recruit from anyone who answers an advert. If you have been to college, you undoubtably have seen posters around the place advertising for participants. You may even have got credits for taking part in research studies. This potentially opens up a large pool of participants, but you still need people to reply to an advert and so you need to make it as attractive as you can and as easy to reply as you can. This used to involve having little tear off strips with phone numbers and email addresses, but now may involve a QR code or something that can be scanned and replied to directly. If you advertise on social media then you can put the link into the tweet, post or story, and given that people are checking out their social media accounts on something that is internet enabled, then they can click straight into any link they see.

This sounds like an easy win, and it certainly can be. It can be a great strategy to recruit a minority group that you belong to and therefore have access to on social media. However, there are things to think about in using this strategy. There is built in bias in recruiting from either adverts within a particular space or via social media. Not everyone goes to college, and not everyone has social media accounts, never mind internet access and computers or smartphones. Furthermore, you are likely to follow and be followed by people with similar demographic features as yourself and therefore you are likely to recruit people with certain demographic features, and these might not be the ones you wanted to recruit. They may not be the best people to answer the question you want to, or they may limit the generalisability of the study you complete. If you cast your net wide, then you might need to screen your participants more carefully prior to them having access to the study procedure. Participants could come from all over the world (see above about language) and they might have lots of different diagnoses and conditions (see above about diagnoses). This means you might have to ask lots of questions of your participants prior to their participation. This might come across as intrusive and might add time and burden to the research procedure.

There are also other ways of getting a general sample. Institutions may collect details of people who are willing to be approached to take part in research. They might have some basic information about these participants, such as their demographics, and/or the kinds of research they are willing to be approached about, and so it might be possible to approach a wider range of participants than your own social media connections or worse, psychology undergraduates. Have a think about what kind of person gives their data to this kind of list, and you will see that you are not getting away from having a biased sample, but it is likely less biased than an undergraduate population!

Data collection services, such as Prolific, recruit a large number of people from around the world to take part in multiple research studies and they pay them for the studies they take part in. With a very large number of people signed up across the world, you can stipulate what characteristics you want your participants to have. The sample may still be biased, and you may need additional screening processes, but it is likely to be much more varied than an undergraduate participant pool. As these participants are being paid then they are likely not to worry about the additional burden of completing screening questions, but the downside is that you will need the funding to do this! These data collection companies facilitate recruitment for online studies. Surveys and self-report measures work well online, and surveys can be well utilised for some kinds of qualitative research. Other cognitive tasks, memory tasks and neuropsychological tasks have been adapted so that they can be used in a virtual research environment. Some research designs of course will not translate to a virtual environment. If you are thinking about using this kind of virtual research world, then reading about the best ways of checking for important aspects of your participants' responses is recommended.

A different approach to open recruitment is to use organisations that have large numbers of potential participants and ask them to invite everyone in the organisation. This is common for research on children where whole classes or even whole schools are invited to send information home to all parents and guardians. This might also be a useful method for recruiting all healthcare workers, or all factory workers, or all gym goers. This approach used to be more common prior to GDPR, but GDPR has prompted us to think more carefully about cold calling people to take part in research. It might be appropriate to invite all children in a school, but is it just as appropriate to invite everyone who has attended a community weight management programme? Services and organisations now may seek consent from their service users to be contacted about research. If you are working within a service and may want to do or support research, this is something you can think about prior to planning research study. This does not mean that people have to take part in research, but it means that they *can* be invited to take part. Recruitment can and should think about equity and inclusion in recruitment procedures and therefore consider who is often excluded from research, directly or indirectly.

Box 2.2: GDPR

GDPR stands for General Data Protection Regulation. It is a regulation brought into effect in the European Union in 2016. It is a response to developments in technology that have been used in the past to use personal data for financial gain and is designed to protect people and uphold their fundamental right (under additional European legislation) from unlawful processing of their personal data.

What is personal data?
Under GDPR **personal data** are data that are related to an identified or identifiable person. However, for the purposes of research it is helpful to think

about this backwards – if your data can identify someone, then it is personal. If you think about the kinds of information we have about people you can see that sometimes it would be quite easy to identify someone (for example if you are someone with both a minority gender and a minority ethnicity in a small sample) and sometimes it would be very difficult to identify someone. Some things are very identifiable, such as names, dates of birth, addresses or email addresses, and voice or video recordings, whereas other things about us are less identifiable, such as our general geography (country or area, urban vs rural etc.), characteristics that make us eligible to take part in the research (for example a particular disease or disorder) or majority gender identity or ethnicity. Sometimes it is not one piece of information about us that makes it identifiable but rather the combination of several pieces of information that can be put together to identify us.

Why is GDPR important to research?

In research, especially psychological research, we process people's personal data. We often ask for people's personal data to identify them, contact them, or for demographics in the write up of the research. In addition, whenever someone is offered an opportunity to write or say their own answer to a question, rather than tick a box or respond to a stimulus, then we are giving them an opportunity to give us personal information.

Is there any research that does not need to consider GDPR?

If there is truly no way for someone to give information that could identify them, for example in a fully anonymous survey with no open text questions, then GDPR does not apply. We still need to consider other ethical issues, such as consent and risk, but we do not need a careful analysis of GDPR risks. The other kind of research that does not require us to consider GDPR is when we are analysing data that has already been collected and fully anonymised. Again, this does not excuse us from ethical considerations, but if the participants are not identifiable then we do not have to consider GDPR principles.

In what way do we have to think about GDPR in psychological research?

Being open about why we are collecting data: If someone is to give informed consent they need to know what we are collecting the data for. This includes what questions we hope to answer, and how we might do the analysis. For most of the research we do, this is easy and standard practice, but there are slight differences if you want to do an experiment where you initially deceive your participants (including not giving them full information); see Chapter 6 for discussion of that. Another example is how we work with interpretation in qualitative analysis where our interpretation of the data might not be how the participants intended their words to be understood. See the chapters on qualitative analysis for more discussion of that.

Getting consent for the processing we are going to do with the data: There are different kinds of bases for processing personal information within the GDP regulations. These are:

Explicit consent
Contract
Legal obligations
Vital interests of the data subject
Public interest
Legitimate interest

Some types of research might invoke the public interest clause for their processing of their personal data, but for most applied psychological research we are going to look for explicit consent.

Only collecting what we need to answer the research question: GDPR asks us to only collect what we need to answer the research question. This doesn't mean absolutely everything we ask needs to be directly tied into the research question – asking about demographic information is crucial for the wider understanding of our research (see Box 2.3), and when we are asking open-ended questions in a qualitative research interview, we understand we can't use every word the person says. However, this part of GDPR means we shouldn't be throwing in another questionnaire just in case. We should think about why we need the information and what we are going to do with it.

Looking after the data well when we have it: Once we have people's personal data it is crucially important that we look after it well. We need to keep it safe, which may include password protection, encryption, locked cabinets (where the keys are not left in the locks) or full anonymisation as early as possible. When we are working within teams we might need to keep track of who is accessing/processing the data and when, in case errors are introduced.

Upholding our participants' rights: Our participants have rights with respect to their data and our processing of it. People can remove their data from our dataset, they can correct it, and they need to know when we are going to destroy the data. Some of these clauses are more for things like health or education records where people might want to update their records or change them or correct errors, but as researchers it is important that we consider these issues too, even if they occur less frequently.

Recruiting from services and organisations

In applied research we often tend to recruit our participants because they access a service or organisation. This allows us to do research that has excellent external validity and that can make a difference, even on a small scale. If we are lucky (and plan well) we can avoid some of the pitfalls of open recruitment with respect to bias, but there are other challenges to recruiting people through a service.

Working with gatekeepers

If you are a student, research assistant or independent researcher, then you might not be embedded within the service you are doing your research in. That means you are likely to be working with gatekeepers. This might involve the gatekeepers giving you access to a clinic where you can talk to potential participants, or gatekeepers sending out letters to potential participants on your behalf, or perhaps the gatekeepers themselves will invite potential participants to take part for you. All of this involves you taking a step back and allowing others to lead on recruitment, even if only the initial stages. This can feel difficult as you no longer have control over one of the most important aspects of your study! It therefore also involves a whole new set of skills in assertiveness and teamwork. At its best, working with a research team ensures good recruitment for the research, thoughtfulness and care for participants, good contextualisation of results and relevance of recommendations arising from the research. At its worst it involves lots of phone-call and email reminders (nagging!), late recruitment (with the stress this causes), and team disengagement from the process and the results. If you have choice, then choosing a good team to work with is a good start. Have they done research with students/research assistants before? And can you talk to them? What did the team do with the results of the research? Was there support all the way through the research from conception, to recruitment, to interpretation and dissemination of results? Are there supports in the organisation for ethical approval applications? Is there any dedicated research support that you can avail of?

Whether or not you have a choice there are things to note when you are initially engaging with a team that can help you determine whether the research is feasible and whether you want to work with this team.

Do they have a clear question that they want asked?

Some teams will feel it is important to do research, but they won't have any specific questions they want answering. This might be useful if you have a question that you want to answer, but you are likely to get less engagement if the question did not arise from their practice.

Do they have a good idea how many participants they might be able to recruit?

When I'm having this conversation with people I try and assess how realistic they are. I want to know how many people the full participant pool is, whether that is the size of the clinic, or the number of children with learning difficulties in a particular school. Then I want to know what proportion of the potential pool of participants the gatekeeper thinks might take part. Reasonable ranges are from 10 per cent (e.g., of all children in a school) to 60/70 per cent (e.g., of people taking part in a psychotherapy group). Sometimes services can predict that 90–100 per cent of the potential participants will take part, but that never really happens. If services have done research in the past, they will have a better idea about how many participants are likely to both consent and then to actually return questionnaires or find time to take part in an interview. If there are only 30 people who can take part from their service, you need to design a study that can work out with as few as 10–15 people.

How do they envisage recruitment happening?

This can be the most stressful part of the research process – handing over control for recruitment of participants to someone else – so it is worth asking lots of questions early in the process. There might be someone whose job it is going to be to ask participants whether they want to take part, such as a research nurse, or a research co-ordinator. This is very helpful, but they might also be recruiting for lots of other studies, and you need to establish a very good relationship with this person so you can ensure good recruitment for your own study. It might be that the service has someone who they will nominate to approach participants, such as the special needs co-ordinator in a school or the head of the professional body for recruitment of those professionals. These people don't have research as their main job, so your research project is likely to be an additional part of a busy job. Anything you can do to make their job easier will both make life better for them, but also maximise your recruitment.

How do the team incorporate research into their practice?

Even if the team have never done research themselves before, it is worth knowing what their relationship with research is. This might involve understanding their motivation for doing research. It might involve finding out whether they engage routinely with research findings, for example with a journal club, or a leadership team that acts on new research findings. If there is research in the service, do they routinely feedback results, and if they do, what do they do with these results? You do not need a team to engage well with research for your research to be completed, but most applied research is designed to improve things for people and knowing how you might be able to do this from the outset can help you make informed decisions about the kind of research you want to do.

Developing working relationships with gatekeepers

Once you have started your research it is your job as the person leading the research to ensure that everyone is kept in the loop about the research. You may need to convene research team meetings. For students, this can be tricky as you may be asking people from a wide range of different backgrounds, and with different timetables, to come together. You are likely to have supervisors from an academic institution working with people within the service. Bringing these people together can be difficult to arrange. There will be different agendas and different expectations across the team, and it is your job to manage these. Having clear agendas for meetings and a clear understanding of the research can be helpful. One aspect of the research that you will develop over time is how much to contact the team. You need to find a balance of making sure that your research project is still on the agenda of the gatekeepers, with making sure you are not nagging. There is no way of determining what is too little or too much contact as every research project is different, but being up front about what your expectations are, and negotiating directly how often to contact people, rather than leaving these things to be implicit, can be helpful. You want to balance keeping the gatekeepers interested and on side, with getting your research completed within a reasonable timeframe. This isn't an optional extra, this is a crucial part of the research process.

Looking after your participants

In the middle of research, especially quantitative research where you need many participants, it can be easy to slip into thinking about participants as things to be counted. However, most applied researchers will need to be thinking about the welfare of their participants throughout the research process, indeed, as a group of mental health service users and carers told me 'do research with us, not to us'. Some of the most meaningful research occurs when engagement happens from the start and the potential participant group is engaged to think about the research from the outset, with input at every stage of the process. However, doing this well takes time and resources, and may be beyond the capacity of the applied researcher especially if you are a student or in training. Either way there are things you can do to prioritise the welfare of your participants throughout. Some of these have been covered above, such as being inclusive in your inclusion criteria, thinking carefully about how to approach participants and asking meaningful questions, but there are additional things to consider.

Balancing the burden of answering questions with answering meaningful questions. GDPR stipulates that we only gather data for a reason. This means we need to think about which questionnaires or tests or interview questions we are including. Many applied researchers err on the side of too few measures. Several studies I have been involved in have got to the end and we wished we had asked an extra measure to help us really understand our data. On the other hand, asking participants to engage in our questionnaires and tests for a long time when we aren't sure exactly what we are going to do with the data risks wasting their time, their emotional energy, and makes the project harder to write up.

Payment of participants. Paying participants can be contentious. It can encourage participation for participants who wouldn't otherwise take part. It can be a suitable thank you for the participant's time. In applied research we often we do not have the resources to pay participants, but there may be other ways to say thank you, such as official reports on their results, or talks or information about help or support for their condition. It is standard to ask participants if they would like a copy of the results of the study, but it is less standard to actually send participants final reports. If you are going to pay participants, think about what a reasonable amount is. Are you giving them a small thank you? Or are you recompensing them for their time? Make sure it is clear up front what you are paying and when.

Making the procedure clear, accessible and pleasant. If possible, it is helpful to let participants know exactly what they are going to do. Give them copies of an interview schedule. Let them have a copy of the questionnaire booklet, or access to it electronically prior to giving consent. During the testing procedure think about what will make the situation best for your participants, including travel, refreshments, lighting, warmth, seating, introductions, and pacing of the procedure itself. Are you going to ask them to stay for the research procedure after a clinic appointment? If so, will this interrupt travel, make parking extremely expensive, or get in the way of childcare? If not, will participants prefer to travel to where they get their care or service, or would they prefer to travel to somewhere more neutral? Are breaks given routinely or only when asked for? What aspects of the procedure can participants have control over, and what can they not choose? During the procedure, if you are meeting with your participants personally, then the quote above can be helpful to keep in mind – 'do research with us, not to us'.

Debriefing. Often a debriefing process involves giving a sheet with phone numbers on it. The phone numbers might be for the research team, or for services that can provide support if the participant is distressed following the research. Often researchers use voluntary organisations on these sheets without checking whether they are suitable or willing to deal with any distress caused. If you are working with a service, it is best to provide both the details of the person within the service who can provide support and also organisations outside of the service that can provide support if the participant does not want to share their distress with the service. You might want to debrief your participants more personally. This is common in qualitative interviews or focus groups where the final questions can act as a debrief process – asking whether there was anything else the participant wanted to add, and asking about how they felt about the interview and whether there was anything they wanted the researcher to pick up on after the interview. However, this can easily be adapted for testing or questionnaire sessions. For some participants and for some topics, it might be that you want to contact your participants sometime after the research procedure, a few days or a week, to see if they are OK with their participation. There might be something they spoke about or answered that has been on their mind, or the interview might have brought up issues that they haven't thought about before and that have stayed on their mind. By contacting them a few days after their participation you can ensure that they are appropriately supported. In our experience, most participants express how positive they found the experience and how glad they were to give of their time to help others, but the ones who are left with a negative feeling are important to engage with.

A final word on gathering demographic and background information on your participants: in all research studies you want to know who has taken part as this can impact how generalisable your results are. It is therefore important to understand who your participants are. As well as asking questions about their gender and age, this might involve asking sensitive questions, including about their race and ethnicity, additional diagnoses, medical history, and disability. With increasing awareness of the lack of generalisability of research due to the systematic exclusion of certain people from research, it is important we ask these questions and do not avoid the ones that might be difficult. Box 2.3 below gives some ideas about minimum demographic information we may wish to ask about.

Box 2.3: Gathering demographic information

Why do we need demographics in research?

Demographic information is a standard part of most reports of psychological research, but how much do we need it and how much attention do we pay to it? Demographic information does something slightly different in quantitative and qualitative research. In quantitative research we need to know who the participants are to determine whether the research is generalisable to the population in question. There is part of this issue that is technical – whenever we do inferential statistical analyses, we make assumptions about what relationship our sample has to the whole population, but there is also part of this issue that is more about our understanding of the research. If we want to know whether an intervention is effective for the clients or patients we work with we might need to know whether it has been tested on people who are like them. If it has only been tested on people who are 18–35, we might not know whether it is effective for people who are 50–80. There are several examples in research where something has been tested on men only (see Caroline Criado-Perez's book, *Invisible Women*, to read all about this) and we know much less about how effective the interventions are for women. Both aspects of generalisability are important when we are determining what demographic information to collect.

In qualitative research demographic information plays a slightly different, albeit overlapping, role. In qualitative research demographic information gives us part of the context for the research. As the unique role all qualitative research plays includes illustrating context and meaning, then understanding context is crucial.

What kinds of demographics might we need?

There is a standard list of demographic variables that are commonly collected in psychological research. These include **gender, age, ethnicity and social economic status (SES)**. However, your research might not need these variables, and other variables might be more important.

In quantitative research we need to know that our participants are a good representative sample of the population we are drawing them from. Therefore, we not only need to know something about our participants, but also about the population. If you are drawing your participants from a rheumatology clinic for example, you might expect them to have a different profile than if you are drawing them from a cystic fibrosis clinic. In both cases we probably need to know participants' ages, gender and/or sex, and ethnicity and race. However, we possibly also want to know the severity of their disease or condition, when they were diagnosed, what kinds of treatments they have had, and perhaps what their exposure to healthcare has been, for example whether they have health insurance or are entitled to free public health care.

In contrast, if we are interested in sleep, then we might be interested, again in age, gender and sex, ethnicity and race, but also in variables that might impact sleep, such as how many people in the household, how many bedrooms, the external environment such as external noise and light, and perhaps indices of poverty that might impact hunger and heating.

All these factors are those that might tell us whether our inferential statistics are valid by being able to compare our sample to the wider population. But when it comes to determining whether the results of a study are relevant to the people we work with, then we might want further information about them. Some of this, such as how they were recruited (were they recruited from an existing service, or did they respond to an open advert?) will be written in the method section, and other details (such as baseline levels of difficulties or of disease activity) might be written in the results. However, by thinking about what information you need to know from a research study when you read it, you can determine what information you might need to collect.

In qualitative research, the challenge is similar, but this time you need to ask yourself: what contextual factors are important for this study? One problem with this is that you might not know until you have collected some or all of the data! There are a number of things that can help you think through what additional contextual information you need about your participants and because you will be inviting your participants to tell you in their own words about their experiences, you can gather this information in an authentic way. You might want to think about the background to the research question and what influenced you to ask this question. You might want to think about the theories that influence your thinking, and you might want to think about papers you have read and what you wanted to know about the participants in those papers.

Further reading

Whelan, R., Cao, Z., O'Halloran, L., & Pennie, B. (2020) Genetics, imaging, and cognition: Big data approaches to addiction research, in A. Verdejo-Garcia (Ed.), *Cognition and Addiction* (pp. 365–377). Cambridge, MA: Academic Press. DOI: https://doi. org/10.1016/B978-0-12-815298-0.00027-7
This chapter has some great practical advice on how to collect your data online. The focus of the researchers is addiction research, but the advice is universal.

Perez, C. C. (2019) *Invisible Women: Data bias in a world designed for men.* New York: Abrams.
This book is essential reading for anyone who thinks science is unbiased. It is the ultimate guide to why we need to think carefully about our participants.

Biros, M. (2018) Capacity, Vulnerability, and Informed Consent for Research. *The Journal of Law, Medicine and Ethics*, 46(1), 72–78. DOI: https://doi.org/10.1177/1073110518766021
This covers key issues in consent for research and assessing capacity.

Bhandari, P. (2022, November 11) Statistical Power and Why It Matters | A Simple Introduction. Scribbr. Retrieved May 26, 2023, from https://www.scribbr.com/statistics/statistical-power/
This is an accessible outline of power, effect sizes and sample sizes with some practical ideas about how to increase the power of your study.

3   Philosophy and theory

How do we know what we know? What is the nature of the knowledge we hold and how we develop that knowledge? What is the nature of truth in psychology? How do knowledge and truth relate to each other? All these questions require us to draw on two related but separate branches of philosophy: epistemology and ontology. Epistemology and ontology are the branches of philosophy concerned with knowledge and truth.

Consider the following statements:

1 The sun came up this morning.
2 The sun comes up every morning.
3 The sun will come up tomorrow morning.
4 Children are generally smart.
5 Smart children do better at school.
6 Children like chocolate.
7 Pain is unbearable.
8 Friendships are hard.
9 Love is like floating on a cloud all day.

As you reflect on these statements, ask yourself:

* How would I go about testing these statements? In other words, how do I create knowledge to support or refute these statements?
* Can I observe something to help me come to this kind of knowledge? And if I can, can it be observed by others?
* If I must do some tests or measurements to know these things, is it clear what tests to do or what measurements to make? Are the results going to be accepted by everyone else or just a sub-set of other people?
* If it isn't testable or measurable, how do I come about this knowledge? Will other people agree with me about this knowledge and if they don't, what value does it have?

Also ask yourself:

* Is this statement true?
* How would I go about showing or proving that this statement is true?
* Who/what is this statement true for?

These are the kinds of questions that help us reflect on our own understanding of the nature of knowledge and truth. Most people will agree that you can test the truth of the first statement and that it is also the one most easily observed. Most people will agree that the last statement is not observable, not testable, and is unique knowledge about someone's experience.

Why is this relevant for psychology? Psychologists need to think about their own assumptions about knowledge and truth because our research does not limit itself to one kind of truth or one kind of knowledge. We are interested in universal nomothetic principles such as whether the amygdala in the brain is responsible for processing threat. However, we are also interested in more idiographic knowledge that helps us understand an individual, such as what the experience of pain feels like for people with unexplained headaches. As applied psychology researchers we may find ourselves being interested in something that isn't easily measured, or that is about personal experiences or opinions. Trying then to make our research fit into more empiricist paradigms where there isn't an objective observable truth might be tricky!

The nature of knowledge and truth is also important because it is political. Assumptions about truth in psychology and other social sciences have not only led to crises about truth and knowledge, such as the replication crisis, but have also led down altogether more dangerous paths, where research findings about different kinds of people based on assumptions about the nature of truth in our research have led to marginalisation, discrimination and worse. Although we are more aware of the danger of some of our assumptions the problem hasn't gone away. We can see this in current examples such as racial biases in AI research, the pushback against genetic research from the autistic community, and in the focus on high achievers in education research about streaming within classes.

The nomothetic and the idiographic

As practitioners we will always be trying to harmonise the idiographic and the nomothetic. That is, we will likely be drawing on research that is based on an assumption that it is generalisable to all people but applying this to an individual person. Most quantitative psychological research uses probabilities to determine its truth. In this kind of research our arbitrary p values of .05 or lower tell us whether something is true or not. There have been great developments in reporting of statistics to get away from this arbitrary arbiter of truth, but we are still dealing with likelihoods and probabilities. If the research says that 60 per cent of people get better with this intervention, then we are going to be happy using that intervention. However, it is hard with the person in front of us to remember that it is still quite likely that the intervention won't work. When it doesn't, we can tend to reject both the intervention and also the research. This isn't a failure of the research – the research never promised it would work for all. It is a failure of our own assumptions about what the research is saying and how we can apply it.

Epistemology

There are lots of ways of creating knowledge and understanding the nature of knowledge created. Indeed, philosophers have been writing about these concepts for centuries. If we look to the history of psychology and how it developed, we see movements from the pragmatism of William James who prioritised how knowledge impacts on people's lives above the more philosophical positions of rationalism or idealism, through Freud's assertion that nothing can truly be known, to Skinner's radical empiricism where only things that can be directly observed and independently measured can be known to be true, to the realist epistemology that characterises the cognitive revolution. It is this realism that permeates much applied psychological research, although we often draw on other aspects of different epistemologies and ontologies when we choose particular research approaches. Two approaches that we often draw on are empiricism, especially for quantitative research, and constructionism, especially for qualitative research. An empiricist approach is one where knowledge is created through experiments. We know the world through our senses, so we observe and experiment with the world to know it better. This contrasts with knowing things through reasoning (rationalism), or through intuition. A constructionist approach is one where knowledge of the world is constructed by the human mind, and therefore, although there might be a reality, our knowledge of it is constructed (and therefore constrained) by the human mind.

One approach is so relevant to applied psychological research that it is worth discussing further, and that is critical realism.

Critical realism and applied psychological research

What is critical realism?

Critical realism is a philosophical position that holds that ontology (nature of reality) is not reducible to epistemology (how knowledge is generated). 'Hard' science, or positivism, would hold that only if we can know something in a certain way can we know reality (the 'epistemic fallacy'). In constructivist constructions of the world, reality is created through human interaction with it, or constructions of it. Both approaches inextricably link the way we know something to the nature of reality. Critical realism suggests that there is a reality that is independent of our knowledge of it, but more than that, it suggests that we can 'know' reality, but it might not be complete, and it can contain errors. Our job as critical realists is to use our best judgement, our critical judgement if you like, to determine what reality is and how confident we are about that.

Pilgrim (2019) explains that the foundations of critical realism are ontological realism, in which the world exists independent of us and our thinking; epistemological relativism, where we construe this world through our own lenses and with our own biases; and judgemental rationalism, where within this real world that we are construing through our own lens, we can weigh up the evidence to come to our own conclusions about what is true and what is real and also about how confident we are about these.

Psychology's reliance on statistics to look at trends and general group find-ings (nomothetical theories and findings) suggest that a positivist approach to knowledge and reality is inadequate for such complex interacting systems. However, most applied psychologists do think about reality and our knowledge of it as being beyond what we construct about it. There may be aspects of our knowledge that do only exist in our construction of it, but that in many other ways there is a reality out there that we can know and that we can come to know through many different ways and lenses. Many applied psychologists would agree that some therapies work better than others, that some people get better with therapy, but others don't, and that there are some general psychological factors that can help us understand people with different kinds of difficulties, but that these are not universal. It is in understanding these uncertainties that we apply our critical thinking and reasoning to determine what is true and how confident we are in that truth. We can be very confident that we know nothing, but we can also be very unconfident about something we do hold to be true.

One of the key tasks of an applied psychologist is to apply our nomothetic theories and research to individuals, therefore taking an idiographic approach. Critical realism as a philosophical position allows us to do this.

The role of theory in applied research

Theory-free research

One of the unique aspects of applied research is that the focus on collecting data can mean that theory isn't needed. Empirical studies that focus on how frequent a phenomenon is in a particular population, such as the prevalence of anxiety in children with dyslexia, or that focus on describing aspects of something, such as common cognitive impairment following stroke, do not require theory to plan or carry out the study. They do not require theory to analyse or interpret the results. These theory-free studies are very valuable to practitioners; they help us argue for more resources, determine where to put the resources we do have, and to understand the parameters that influence our work.

One example of a theory-free research approach that is widely used in applied psychology is audit. An audit can be a very useful way of making changes in a service. The *audit cycle* describes the stages of an audit, which are determin-ing our goals, testing how we are doing in relation to these goals, and planning how to get closer to them. It is a cyclical process, as any progress made towards the goals needs to be measured, and new plans made. When the goals are met it might be that the audit process can determine whether the goal is maintained. Maintaining a goal might also require active plans to ensure it happens. An example is auditing health service waiting lists. Waiting list goals might be set external to the service, perhaps by governmental or professional bodies, or it might be set by the service itself. Data is gathered to check how close the

Figure 3.1 An audit cycle

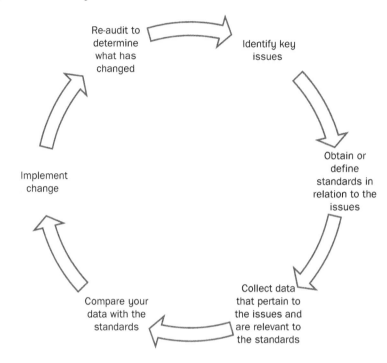

Re-audit to determine what has changed

Identify key issues

Obtain or define standards in relation to the issues

Implement change

Collect data that pertain to the issues and are relevant to the standards

Compare your data with the standards

service is to meeting the goals. This leads to certain plans or interventions to improve waiting times. These plans are carried out, and then data is gathered again to see if the waiting times have decreased (improved). The plans/interventions needed to reduce a very long waiting list might be quite different to those needed to reduce a short waiting list, which might be quite different to those needed to maintain a suitable waiting list. The cycle however, continues.

Quality in theory-free research

Some of the key aspects of quality in theory-free research are relevant to all research. Whether the research is driven by or interpreted using theory, it is important that the question asked is aligned with the methods used to answer it and the analysis strategy – this is described more in Chapter 1 and in the individual methods chapters. Secondly, no matter what kind of research you are doing you should think about the quality of the data you collect. This involves:

Choosing a good way to collect data. This might be well validated questionnaires, surveys designed specifically for the research project, interviews, focus groups or analysis of existing data.

Making sure that the data collected answers the question. There is something very appealing in using data that is already available, such as standard intake questionnaires for a service, or national test scores, but if these do not answer your question then they you may need to collect additional data. It may also sometimes feel that it is best to design a new survey from scratch because then you can ask exactly what you want. This can be highly effective but reduces reliability as you will not have any information on test–retest reliability, inter-rater or inter-informant reliability, and it may be difficult to test internal consistency and factor structure with smaller numbers of participants.

Minimising missing data. This can involve thinking about the participation burden on the participants to ensure they get to the end of the study. It may involve offering breaks or breaking up the data collection into several sessions. It may involve sitting with participants to complete the measures or putting them online where you can set up your system to alert participants when they have not completed a question. It may also involve having systems in place to input relevant data with training for other members of the team in how to do this. Many a research project has gone wrong when some members of the team input their dates the UK way (date, month, year), and some input their dates the US way (month, date, year).

The third thing to plan for is to get appropriate participants to take part. Again, this is multi-faceted and is described in more detail in Chapter 2. It involves having the right number of participants for the study design, considering homogeneity or heterogeneity of participants (depending on what the design calls for), and making sure that both visible and invisible aspects of diversity are asked about so that it is clear who the results refer to. Finally, good research should be appropriately contextualised. One of the differences between theory-free research and theory driven research may be in its scope and how far we might expect it to be generalisable. Theory-free research should always provide sufficient contextual information, not only about the participants, but about the wider context from which they are drawn, for readers to be able to make judgements about what the results mean.

Theory in applied psychological research

There is an interesting role for theory in applied psychological research. There are strong roots of psychology in empiricism and experimental methods. These draw largely on ideas of theory from scientific paradigms. In science, theory explains phenomena and predicts outcomes. It can be tested and proven wrong. When data is collected that contradicts it, we should put the theory aside. In social science this doesn't work. Our systems are too complicated. We determine the truth of our experiments using arbitrary statistical cut-off points and we work with phenomena that cannot be directly observed or measured. Thus, the role of theory in social science is somewhat different. Most would agree that theories describe and go beyond descriptions to explain. In social science, theories are mostly in narrative form, and they seek to account for variation in phenomena, either by contextualising the phenomena in question, or by putting limits and boundaries round what the theory describes. The rise of qualitative research that draws more on constructionist philosophies and involves more subjective researcher interpretation has meant that applied psychology has had to embrace its social science perspective and loosen its association with tight scientific conceptualisations of theory.

Psychological research can create theories, can develop existing theories and can test theories. The role theory plays in research can depend on the research method being used and the analysis strategy employed. In much quantitative research, theory drives our hypotheses, it drives our choice of which variables to include and maybe which variables not to include, it drives our choice of analysis, determining whether we look at associations, group differences, change over time or mediators and moderators. In qualitative research, theory can guide the direction of our study, including the questions we ask of our participants. It can guide the very qualitative approach we take to collect and analyse our data, and it can guide our understanding of what we find.

Box 3.1: Theories, frameworks and models

Construct	Describe or explain?	Size and scope	Role of contextual factors
Theory	Both	Variable, can be big or small, specific or general depending on explanatory value of the theory	Determined by what it is a theory about
Framework	Describe	Typically large. This sacrifices detail, but a framework gives a good overview of key categories and broadly how they are related	Incorporated in the framework
Model	Describe	Typically small. Models should describe well a specific set of constructs within a limited context and how they are related to each other	Not often made explicit

In the chapters on different methods, you will see that theory is embedded in the research decisions we take. It is perhaps most evident when we are using large datasets to test our hypotheses. In these large datasets we can take into account many different variables, and thus test whole models or theories. We often have large enough sample sizes to explore the relationships between all the variables in a particular theory, rather than limit ourselves to testing associations between two or three. However, even when we aren't working with a large dataset, we are often influenced by a model or theory (see Box 3.1 for a description of differences between theories, models and frameworks). The theory might tell us which variables are most important. It might tell us how we expect the variables to relate to each other. As well as theory being important in developing our ideas, theory is important in interpreting our findings. Theory can help us feel that our research is relevant beyond the small number of participants who took part. It can help us develop ideas that might be helpful to our participant population that build on the similarities between our findings and the findings of others.

Further reading

Pilgrim, D. (2019) *Critical Realism for Psychologists* (1st ed.). Abingdon: Routledge. DOI: https://doi.org/10.4324/9780429274497
A perfect book to help you understand critical realism and its role in psychological research.

Scotland, J. (2012) Exploring the philosophical underpinnings of research: Relating ontology and epistemology to the methodology and methods of the scientific, interpretive, and critical research paradigms. *English Language Teaching*, 5(9), p9. DOI: https://doi.org/10.5539/elt.v5n9p9
This is a shorter paper that describes some key terms I have used in this chapter.

4 | Systematic reviews

Applied psychological research is going on all the time all over the world. There are hundreds of journals that publish thousands of papers each month. That is a lot of research. Our first stop if we want to answer an applied psychological research question should be to see if someone else has done it first. This saves us time, effort, resources, and perhaps most importantly of all, it saves our participants the time and emotional labour of taking part in research. How much research never gets disseminated? How much time has been wasted doing research, both from the researchers' and participants' perspectives?

However, when we do go to the published research there are all kinds of difficulties with it. We might not find research on the population we are interested in. We might not be able to trust the findings due to poor quality research. Other researchers might have answered different questions that partially answer our own research question, but not completely. Finally, there may be studies that contradict each other, and it might be hard to work out which one to trust.

One solution to these problems is to review the literature in a systematic way.

NB: Systematic Reviews (capital S, capital R) are a specific way of systematically reviewing the literature with their own methods, techniques and proponents. This chapter takes a broader understanding of what a systematic review (small s, small r) is, therefore, there may be differences between what you find in this chapter and other writing on Systematic Reviews.

What is this approach?

A systematic review tries to systematically find all the papers that answer our research question, and then to synthesise all the results. This allows us to determine what we know about a particular topic, what the gaps are in the literature and what the limits are to generalisability of findings.

There are lots of different ways of reviewing literature all with their own pros and cons (see Box 4.1 for a list of some of them), but all of them take a systematic approach to finding research literature that answers your research question and a robust and systematic approach to summarising and/or synthesising the literature.

Philosophy

Most systematic reviews are empiricist by nature. They assume a reality that can be found by combining lots of research studies. The reasoning involved is abductive reasoning, whereby we combine inductive reasoning, focused on developing our understanding of the data, with deductive reasoning focused on finding evidence about aspects of the questions we are asking. Combining these two kinds of reasoning gives us the best answer to our complex, real-life questions. Critical realism is also apparent in the philosophy of many systematic reviews, where the evidence is reviewed critically as well as being synthesised. Finally, there is a place for constructionism in qualitative systematic reviews much as meta-syntheses.

What kind of questions are best answered using this method?

Lots of different kinds of questions can be answered using systematic reviews. Some reviews are designed to give an overarching answer to a question, such as 'does this intervention work?' or 'are these two constructs associated with each other?'. Others are designed to give an overview of what research has been done on the topic. Reviews and literature syntheses can be used to create new understandings of the literature by synthesising the literature and providing a wider context for this than a single study.

What are the key steps to using this method?

Work out your question. If your study has been prompted by a clinical or practical curiosity, this might be quite easy. You know what you want to know. However, it might be that you have to complete a systematic review for a qualification, and that isn't so easy! You need to make sure no-one else has done it, you need to choose something that is the right size to complete in the time available, and you need to choose something that is aligned with your own area of practice. Either way, there are some steps you can do to develop your question.

Write down what you want to know and discuss this with your research team to hone your idea.

Check that your question hasn't already been answered in a good systematic review. Chapter 1 gives more detail on how to do this, but check out Google Scholar, key review journals and perhaps a relevant academic search engine (Cinahl, PsychInfo, PubMed etc.) using your research question or your key terms. If you find something that looks like it answers your research question, then read it carefully to check whether it is a good review of the literature. Things you might look for are the breadth of the search terms, the papers that were included with a good account of what was not included and why, clear descriptions of the papers that were included (usually in a table), a good synthesis of the included literature rather than just a list of what each study did, and reasonable conclusions. If it is a meta-analysis, then check out the statistics (perhaps with someone with specialist statistical expertise) and the inclusion and exclusion criteria as these can significantly affect the results. If the review does answer the question you had, then either this is great news – you can take it back into your workplace, perhaps discuss at a journal club, or disseminate to colleagues, or it is a disaster, because you have to do a review, and someone has already done it! If that is the case, then read the review carefully (again), and go back to step one to determine what else the research team wants to know about the topic.

Scope out your question. Although there are systematic reviews with hundreds of papers (e.g., Swift & Greenberg, 2012) and a very small number with no papers at all (see Chapman et al., 2022 or Townend et al., 2008), to complete a systematic review in a reasonable timeframe without a huge research group, you need a goldilocks-sized review question. It is no good reviewing four papers (unless the arguments for doing so are indisputable), and you are going to struggle to review four hundred papers. There isn't an optimum number of papers or studies to include – you need to include as many as is needed to answer the question and you need to be guided by your question rather than the literature. Having said this, there are ways to narrow your research question in order that a synthesis of the literature makes sense. For example, can you restrict your participants by including papers only with elite athletes or amateur athletes? Can you restrict your search to certain methodologies, such as only including longitudinal papers or only experimental papers? Finally, can you restrict an aspect of the question, for example if you are interested in executive functioning in anxious children, can you focus in on one important aspect of executive functioning, such as attention switching?

Box 4.1: Types of systematic review and the kinds of questions they answer

Type of review	What it is	What kinds of research questions it answers
Literature review	Literature reviews are overviews of a body of literature. They are mainly used as introductions to wider works, such as theses, dissertations, or monographs. Typically, they are written by an expert in the field, who gained expertise either through intensive study (PhD students, etc.) or through a lifetime of work (research experts). They are also often 'funnel-shaped'; that is, they start with a broad introduction to the topic and narrow down to key issues that are then explored further.	Literature reviews are not usually guided by a research question beyond 'What do we know about this topic?'. Their function is more in relation to what comes next in the writing and setting up a clear argument, rather than answering a question by itself.

Type of review	What it is	What kinds of research questions it answers
Narrative review	A narrative review synthesises the available literature into a coherent narrative on the topic. Narrative reviews have typically been seen as an extension of literature reviews and therefore considered lesser as they have less 'scientific' or structured methodology. However, researchers including Greenhalgh argue that there is a very important role for narrative reviews because instead of answering a narrow question they provide 'interpretation and critique'.	As narrative reviews can put together diverse literature on a topic, the best questions are those that address a relevant question to practitioners and that deepen our understanding of that topic. These can be narrow or broad and draw on a variety of methodologies.
Rapid review	A rapid review takes on the main stages in a review but does it quickly! In order to do a review in less time, something has to be shortened. This can partially be done by having a narrow question. However, it can also be done by limiting the searches – they are still done systematically and described fully transparently, but they may be more limited in scope. It can be done by limiting the synthesis or by the quality appraisal.	Questions that are best answered by rapid reviews are those where an answer is required quickly. For example, at the start of the COVID-19 pandemic a review on the effectiveness of mask wearing needed to be done quickly! A review that took 2–3 years was not going to help public policy or practice!
Scoping review	Scoping reviews determine the scope of the literature. They can tell us how many studies/papers there are on a topic, as well as the kinds of methods these studies use and to identify gaps in the literature. They can be used as a precursor to a systematic review.	Scoping review questions usually ask what we know about a topic, but they may have a slightly narrower focus, such as what research has been completed on a topic, or they may focus on one aspect of the studies such as the methods used in a field or the variety of populations the field encompasses.

Type of review	What it is	What kinds of research questions it answers
Integrative review	An integrative review takes all the evidence on a topic and synthesises it in order to draw conclusions. It is inclusive of a wide variety of studies and is not restricted by the methods used in these studies. It weighs up the evidence from the studies in terms of their quality and what the methods can and cannot prove. It can be very similar to a good narrative review but with a greater focus on including all the relevant literature, and it can be similar to a scoping review but with a greater emphasis on drawing conclusions.	Integrative reviews ask the same kinds of questions as narrative reviews. They should have relevance for practice or be a topic of interest, and there should be benefits for understanding the topic of including a diverse range of studies.
Systematic review	Systematic review is something of an umbrella term in the literature. Some people use it interchangeably with meta-analysis, although a meta-analysis always does the statistical analysis, whereas a systematic review doesn't. Some people contrast systematic reviews with other kinds of review, even though many other types of review take a systematic approach to finding and synthesising the literature. My understanding of a systematic review is that there is a strong attempt to systematically find all the literature, systematically extract relevant data, and then systematically synthesise this data.	Because systematic reviews and meta-analyses have had such a close relationship, systematic reviews sometimes address more narrow questions than narrative or integrative reviews. They may be looking for a more certain kind of conclusion rather than a greater depth of understanding. For example, we might want to know what kinds of interventions work for hyperactive children in the classroom, rather than asking the broader question about what interventions there are, do they work, how, and how are they received?

Type of review	What it is	What kinds of research questions it answers
Meta-analysis	A meta-analysis is a way of combining the statistics of lots of quantitative studies to determine an overall effect. For this effect to be accurate it is crucially important to identify all the relevant studies, and therefore the basis of a meta-analysis is a strong systematic search for the literature, and reliable extraction of data from papers.	A meta-analysis requires a simple quantitative question that can be answered with one (or maybe a few) finding(s). For example, do older adults who fall have poor depth perception? Sometimes within a meta-analysis it is possible to do sub-group analyses or a meta-regression, so that you could ask whether age impacts the relationship between falling and depth perception in older adults. A meta-analysis also works best when the studies are not too different from each other (not too heterogenous), so some questions are not good for meta-analysis because the research methods chosen to study them in the primary studies are so varying it is like comparing apples and oranges, and in some cases, like comparing apples and staplers.

Type of review	What it is	What kinds of research questions it answers
Realist review	A realist review aims to find out how things work and what the mechanisms are. Unlike other reviews that mainly focus on reviewing the existing studies, realist reviews involve a whole research team with different stakeholders being involved. It involves engagement with the literature and what it means in real life, and a wider conception of what the evidence consists of. A realist review is the review type most likely to actively seek grey literature and non-academic studies.	The best kinds of questions for a realist review are 'how' questions. These reviews ask how things work in real life.
Meta-synthesis	A meta-synthesis is a review of qualitative studies where the findings of each are combined, usually using some kind of thematic or framework analysis.	The kinds of questions best asked using meta-synthesis are similar to those best asked using qualitative methods. These include questions like 'what are people's experiences of...?' 'what are the meanings people give to ...?' and 'what is the lived experience of people with condition/ disorder x?'

Type of review	What it is	What kinds of research questions it answers
Meta-ethnography	A meta-ethnography takes a meta-synthesis one step further. Where a meta-synthesis takes qualitative papers and looks for commonalities using more realist or post-positivist approaches to qualitative analysis, meta-ethnography takes qualitative studies and analyses them using a more constructionist/reflexive qualitative approach. In a meta-ethnography the frequency of themes across the papers is not of interest, and the aim is not a reduction of themes into relevant categories, but rather a new analysis revealing a new understanding of a topic.	The same kind of questions that can be answered using meta-synthesis can be answered using meta-ethnography. The main difference is the methods used rather than the questions asked. The aim in a meta-ethnography is to develop a new understanding rather than a more realist synthesis of the literature and therefore you want to check whether you want this new understanding and whether the literature is appropriate for developing it.

Work out the parameters of your search

What are your search terms? These might interact with your search engines, as some search engines have expansion terms – that is once you enter a particular term you can include or exclude other terms associated with it. However, you need to determine key search terms for each aspect of your question, with synonyms for each of them. It can be helpful to use a framework such a PICOS or SPIDER to help with this (see Methley et al., 2014).

What are your inclusion and exclusion criteria? These determine what you will include in your review and what you will not. These are likely to be refined as you go along, as each systematic review throws up new issues, but you might have a good idea from the start the key things you want to include and want to exclude. These are likely to align themselves with your search terms but limit them further. For example, if you search for 'parent' you might want to include studies that only have biological parents as participants. If you search for 'older adult' you might want the mean age of your participants to be over 65, or you might exclude any studies with any participants under the age of 65.

Which search engines are you going to use? There may be obvious ones in your field such as PsychInfo in psychology, PubMed for anything health or medicine related, and Social Sciences Full Text for wider social science topics. There are general search engines such as Web of Science or Scopus that can be helpful but can also give you a lot of irrelevant papers. Google Scholar has a different way of searching and so should be used in a different way than the other search engines, but can be a useful addition or useful for including the grey literature.

What dates are you going to include? In general, I would recommend not having specific dates that limit your search. Arbitrarily choosing a date to restrict the number of papers, or only reviewing papers added since a previous review impacts the validity of your conclusions. The circumstances in which it might be reasonable to restrict your dates is if there has been a significant change to diagnosis, to legislation, or to treatment/practice that would impact the literature significantly. For example, if you wanted to review experiences of getting consent from people with intellectual disabilities you might want to only include literature from after legislation enshrining their rights to do this was introduced and enacted.

Register your review. This means committing to answering a particular question in a particular way and sticking to it! There are lots of good reasons to register your review, including it being good science and encouraging you to think through your procedure very carefully before you start, encouraging you to complete the review, but it is also helpful to others who might be trying to do something similar. If you know someone else is doing the review it might help you choose a different question or a different way of answering the question. This theoretically reduces duplication and encourages transparency more widely in research.

Now you are ready to **find the papers that will go into your review**. Usually this is a four-step process:

1 Put your search terms into your search engine and get a list of all the papers that include them.
2 Download them into a reference manager and remove duplicates. These are the papers that were found by more than one of the search engines.
3 Review each title and abstract to see if it meets your inclusion criteria. If it does, keep it for the next step, and if it doesn't, note a reason why. If you are searching through thousands of papers, it may not be necessary to keep a reason for the exclusion of each paper at this stage, rather it might be worth keeping track of key reasons for exclusion.
4 Review the full text of each paper. Read the method (and possibly results for a qualitative synthesis) of the study in detail to determine whether it meets your inclusion criteria. At this stage it is worth keeping detailed notes about why particular papers were excluded. This helps with the audit trail for any other members of the research team, it is good to report in the write up, and it clarifies for you the kinds of studies that aren't making it into the final synthesis. This is the step that you are most likely to try and get inter-rater reliability statistics for.

There are some additional stages that you might want to consider:

- You might want to exclude papers that don't meet certain quality criteria (see below for quality ratings).
- You might want to search your included papers' reference lists for possible additional studies to include.
- You might want to search the papers that have cited your included papers to see if there are any of those studies to include (forward searching).
- You might want to hand search certain key journals to see if any papers have been missed.

The next step is often a **quality rating** of the studies you are including. By assessing how good the studies are that you are including you can make more certain judgements about your conclusions based on them. Some aspects of quality might be considered in your inclusion and exclusion criteria, for example, only included randomised controlled trials in your meta-analysis. Other aspects, such as sample size, methodology, statistical appropriateness, and accuracy of conclusions drawn might influence how you include your studies. There are a lot of different tools for assessing quality in different kinds of studies, and a lot of recommendations out there as to how to use them. The Joanne Briggs Institute critical appraisal tools (https://jbi.global/critical-appraisal-tools) are a good place to start for many reviews of psychological studies. You need to find a quality assessment tool that fits your own needs, both in terms of the studies you are going to include in your own synthesis, and also that assesses the aspects of the study that are important to your question. A quality assessment tool for a meta-analysis might be quite different to a quality assessment tool for a meta-ethnography.

Extract the data. It might be relatively straightforward what data you want to extract. For example, for a meta-analysis you will need numbers of participants, outcome data, and data to contextualise the samples. However, for a broader review it might be harder to determine what data to extract. You will have to make decisions about what constitutes data. Is it anything in the results section? Is it anything that the participant has contributed, whether that is a score on a questionnaire or a direct quote? Is it anything that arises directly from the procedure that can help answer your research question? Most reviews will involve charting the data extracted, for example with key columns for year of publication, country of publication, number of participants, method/measures, and main findings, with possible open-ended columns at the end for notes. Sometimes you will want to get inter-rater reliability on the extraction of your data, especially for meta-analyses, but other times just having someone audit part of your data extraction can be sufficient.

Synthesise the data. This is where the different methods diverge most significantly. With a meta-analysis you will be synthesising the data quantitatively. With a narrative analysis you will be synthesising the data in meaningful chunks. With a meta-ethnography you will be synthesising the data to develop a new understanding of the topic, and with a scoping review the synthesis itself is likely to be minimal, with a focus on description. Synthesis of literature can be harder than it looks. It takes time and cognitive effort. It is very common at the start to not see any patterns in the data and to only see the differences. This can lead to lists of descriptions of individual papers. I wouldn't worry if you do this – it can be a key part of the process that you have to go through to get to where you want to be, which is somewhere where you can bring different findings together to create new knowledge based on larger numbers or on diverse populations, or by combining different study methods. However, this stage is where your research team is invaluable.

Write your findings up justifying your research decisions at each stage, being as transparent as you can about the process, and working hard to synthesise, not simply describe, your findings. Try and go beyond the cliché of 'more research is needed' to pull out key implications for future research. If more research is needed, why and what kinds of research? In terms of practice recommendations, make sure you are basing these on your findings, not on your own preconceived ideas of what should be done. If the literature is mixed as to its conclusions, own this rather than ignoring the studies that don't fit. This is why you have done a systematic review after all!

How does this method usually go wrong and what can you do about it?

If you get as far as identifying a suitable question, then the main issues that are common in systematic reviews are poor choice of studies, leading to erroneous conclusions through biased selection of papers, problems with the papers found making it hard to synthesise the information in a useful way, and poor synthesis of papers that are found. To deal with these problems you need to ensure you have inclusion and exclusion criteria that only include the studies good enough to be included. You need to have good alignment between your question and the type of review chosen. For example, you might want to review interventions for falling in older adults. If you want to see what kinds of interventions have been developed, what the active ingredients are, and what kinds of effects, including satisfaction with the intervention, are found, then simple designs, such as pre–post designs or single case designs may be suitable to include. However, if you want to see if a particular intervention is better than an active control, you are likely to need to include only randomised controlled trials and use a meta-analytic approach. Good alignment also means you will avoid erroneous conclusions based on poor evaluation of assumptions. For example, in a meta-analysis you can control for different size studies with different size effects, potentially from different populations. If in a narrative review you simply count the number of papers with p values less than .05 and compare them to the number of papers with p values more than .05, then you are likely to make erroneous conclusions as each study will be impacted by different sample sizes, different measures, etc. It is possible to compare effect sizes in a narrative review as these are not as arbitrary as p values, but as soon as you want to make firm conclusions about things being effective, or one thing being more effective than another, then these are quantitative questions, and you need to take a quantitative approach to answering them.

You can partially address the issue of having too much variation in your studies to be able to usefully synthesise them by choosing the correct kind of review, and by scoping out your review prior to committing to it. For example, synthesising a wide variety of methods in studies is pretty much impossible using meta-analysis, but completely reasonable in a scoping or critical review. In order to do a good synthesis, you will need to have sufficient time to read the papers many times and to think about how the results fit together. This might involve finding time to work with your research team or write drafts for colleagues or supervisors to review. Often, we are working to a deadline, but time is required for a good synthesis to come together.

What are the practical issues associated with this method?

The main practical issues associated with doing reviews is finding the papers you need for the review. If you have an institutional affiliation, then you are likely to be able to find appropriate papers for your review. Most journals have got electronic copies of most papers that are available via searchable databases. However, getting access to papers may include physically going into a library to copy papers from the physical journal, or even applying for inter-library loans!

There are alternative ways of sourcing the papers you need to review, including checking Google Scholar, checking with the author directly, either on their own webpage (personal or institutional), via professional networking sites like LinkedIn or ResearchGate, or by emailing the person directly. The older the paper, the less likely it is that you'll be able to source your papers this way, but it is always worth trying.

If you don't have an institutional affiliation (some hospitals will have access to these kinds of resources), then this will be difficult. You can source papers individually and pay for each of them, but you may reject many of them at full text review stage and therefore it can seem like a waste of money. It is much easier to find someone to work with who does have access to the databases and libraries you need.

There are some practical issues that can arise from working on a large systematic review that are related to project management and making sure that everyone does their tasks within a reasonable timeframe, but this isn't a research issue per se, rather a project management issue.

Ethics

There are few ethical issues to consider when completing a systematic review. If you are reviewing already published data, then it can be argued that this is a good use of the participants' and researchers' time and effort. The main consideration is about the quality of the review. I'm writing this after years of COVID-19 restrictions and these years have been littered with poor meta-analyses and systematic reviews. There have of course been excellent meta-analyses and systematic reviews in that time too, but when we need up-to-date scientific information, a poor review or meta-analysis could have a disproportionate influence on policy and practice. It is an ethical imperative to do good research, but reviews are taken very seriously by others and therefore this imperative is strong in the field of reviews.

Example: Responding to a call for papers: Developing a focused research project

Reynolds, S., Wilson, C., Austin, J. & Hooper, L. (2012). Effects of psychotherapy for anxiety in children and adolescents: A meta-analytic review, *Clinical Psychology Review*, 32(4), 251–262. DOI: 10.1016/j. cpr.2012.01.005

This project started because of a call for papers in a journal with a high impact factor and lots of relevant studies in it. A call for papers happens when a journal wants to put together a collection of papers on a theme or a special issue. The call was for research on the parameters of what works in terms of interventions for child anxiety. Shirley Reynolds and I both had an interest in anxiety in childhood, and we both had an interest in CBT and its adaptations. We both knew, from our experience of talking about CBT for anxious children, that contrary to popular belief at the time, there were a lot of studies of CBT for anxious children – so many that it might be possible to delineate some important parameters that determine how the therapy should look rather than simply answer the question 'does CBT work?'. This had been answered really well already by two independent groups of researchers (Cartwright-Hatton, et al., 2004; James et al., 2007), but from the start, we were interested in whether including parents was important, whether the number of sessions was important, whether including exposure was important, etc. The plan was always to look at what works better rather than to answer a simple question about whether therapy does work.

In the process of designing the study we had some interesting choices to make. First, we had to ask whether we were only interested in CBT or whether we were interested in all psychotherapy. As clinical psychologists, we understood not all children responded well to CBT, and that not all practitioners were keen on using CBT. Therefore, we decided quite easily that we were interested in all psychotherapies. The second decision was what we were going to include as anxiety. At the time, the DSM listed the anxiety disorders as Generalised Anxiety Disorder, Panic Disorder, Agoraphobia, Specific Phobia, Social Phobia, Obsessive-Compulsive Disorder, Posttraumatic Stress Disorder, and Acute Stress Disorder, with Separation Anxiety Disorder being classified as a(n) Other Disorder of Infancy, Childhood or Adolescence. Most of the CBT studies we were aware of focused on Separation Anxiety Disorder, Generalised Anxiety Disorder, and Social Phobia. Some of the studies included children with Specific Phobias. When trials included children with anxiety disorders, they generally didn't include children with OCD or PTSD. However, we also knew that there were several studies that did include children with just these diagnoses. So, after several conversations, we decided we wanted to be broad in our focus. We would risk there not being a coherent story to tell at the benefit of being more inclusive. We decided, over the course of these conversations, that not only would we include studies that recruited children with any of these anxiety disorders, but also that we would include studies where children did not have diagnosed anxiety disorders but were recruited because of elevated scores on an anxiety symptoms questionnaire. These kinds of decisions must be made carefully. If the papers you include are too varied, then you risk not being able to make any conclusions. However, we made a clear decision to include everything we could, and to try and evaluate and describe some of the nuance in that.

Further reading

There are lots of websites and papers that will step you through how to do a systematic review. Most of them are helpful, so find one that suits you! These references might point to more specific issues.

Books

Onwuegbuzie, J. A. & Frels, R. (2016) *Seven Steps to a Comprehensive Literature Review.* Thousand Oaks, CA: Sage Publications.
This focuses on synthesising mixed methods studies in a review, but that means it is appropriate for lots of the review types mentioned in the above table.

Borenstein, M., Hedges, L. V., Higgins, J. P. T. & Rothstein, H. R. (2021) *Introduction to Meta-analysis* (2nd ed.). New York: John Wiley & Sons Ltd.
The bible of meta-analysis and (relatively) accessible!

Finfgeld-Connett, D. (2018) *A Guide to Qualitative Meta-synthesis.* Abingdon: Routledge.
This is a lovely straightforward guide on how to do a qualitative meta-synthesis

Noblit, G. W. & Hare, R. D. (1988) *Meta-ethnography: Synthesising qualitative studies.* London: Sage Publications.
The original and the best. Some of the language is technical, but a must read for anyone doing a meta-ethnography.

Websites

Temple University Guide to review types.
https://guides.temple.edu/c.php?g=78618&p=3879604
This is worth checking to see which review best answers your research question.
UK-based register of systematic reviews
https://www.crd.york.ac.uk/prospero/

Papers

Akers, J., Aguiar-Ibáñez, R., & Baba-Akbari, A. (2009). Systematic reviews: CRD's guidance for undertaking reviews in health care. Centre for Reviews and Dissemination, University of York https://www.york.ac.uk/media/crd/Systematic_Reviews.pdf.

Arksey, H., & O'Malley, L. (2005). Scoping studies: Towards a methodological framework. *International Journal of Social Research Methodology*, 8(1), 19–32. DOI: https://doi.org/10.1080/1364557032000119616

Greenhalgh, T., Thorne, S., & Malterud, K. (2018). Time to challenge the spurious hierarchy of systematic over narrative reviews? *European Journal of Clinical Investigation*, 48(6). DOI: https://doi.org/10.1111/eci.12931

Munn, Z., Peters, M. D. J., Stern, C., Tufanaru, C., McArthur, A., & Aromataris, E. (2018). Systematic review or scoping review? Guidance for authors when choosing between a systematic or scoping review approach. *BMC Medical Research Methodology*, 18(1). DOI: https://doi.org/10.1186/s12874-018-0611-x

Pawson, R., Greenhalgh, T., Harvey, G., & Walshe, K. (2005). Realist review—A new method of systematic review designed for complex policy interventions. *Journal of Health Services Research & Policy*, 10(1_suppl), 21–34. DOI: https://doi.org/10.1258/1355819054308530

Saul, J. E., Willis, C. D., Bitz, J., & Best, A. (2013). A time-responsive tool for informing policy making: Rapid realist review. *Implementation Science*, 8(1), 103. DOI: https://doi.org/10.1186/1748-5908-8-103

Swift, J. K., & Greenberg, R. P. (2012). Premature discontinuation in adult psychotherapy: A meta-analysis. *Journal of Consulting and Clinical Psychology*, 80(4), 547–559. DOI: https://doi.org/10.1037/a0028226

Chapter references

Cartwright-Hatton, S., Roberts, C., Chitsabesan, P., Fothergill, C., & Harrington, R. (2004). Systematic review of the efficacy of cognitive behaviour therapies for childhood and adolescent anxiety disorders. *British Journal of Clinical Psychology*, 43(4), 421–436. https://doi.org/10.1348/0144665042388928

Chapman, L., Hutson, R., Dunn, A., Brown, M., Savill, E., & Cartwright-Hatton, S. (2022). The impact of treating parental anxiety on children's mental health: An empty systematic review. *Journal of Anxiety Disorders*, 88, 102557.

James, A., Soler, A., & Weatherall, R. (2007). Cochrane review: Cognitive behavioural therapy for anxiety disorders in children and adolescents. *Evidence-Based Child Health: A Cochrane Review Journal*, 2(4), 1248–1275. https://doi.org/10.1002/ebch.206

Methley, A. M., Campbell, S., Chew-Graham, C., McNally, R., & Cheraghi-Sohi, S. (2014). PICO, PICOS and SPIDER: A comparison study of specificity and sensitivity in three search tools for qualitative systematic reviews. *BMC Health Services Research*, 14(1). DOI: https://doi.org/10.1186/s12913-014-0579-0

Townend, M., Tew, J., Grant, A., & Repper, J. (2008). Involvement of service users in education and training: A review of the literature and exploration of the implications for the education and training of psychological therapists. *Journal of Mental Health*, 17(1), 65–78.

5 Using large and existing datasets

Sometimes someone else has done the hard work of collecting data for you. Using existing databases can answer questions that any small study that an applied scientist does is unlikely to be able to. They can do this by having sufficient participants to answer large-scale questions. Useful questions can be asked of routine clinical information collected systematically, or from very large community studies. If the main advantage of using this data for you, the researcher, is the number and representation of participants, then the main disadvantage is that the person or people collecting the data might not have collected the data you really want. However, it is worth thinking about the advantages for the participants as well. By collecting data that can be used to answer multiple questions, participants' time and energy are being well used. Furthermore, by increasing representation in the data, either through routine collection of it (in services) or by collecting data in a way that maximises the representation of participants (in epidemiological studies), it is possible to answer questions about minority populations that are difficult to recruit, and that are therefore often ignored, or worse, excluded, from smaller studies.

What is this approach?

Using a large and/or existing dataset is not a specific research method. You need to determine what method you are going to use to analyse the data, but there are some approaches that work better depending on what data has been collected. Some of it might be collected with an intervention or some kind of experimental manipulation in between two data time points, but most datasets will be collected with no manipulation. Therefore, you are mainly looking for relationships between your variables (check out Chapter 9) or differences between groups (check out Chapter 8). Often epidemiological studies collect data at repeated time points, and so changes over time can be captured.

A thorough review and explanation of different statistical analysis methods that can be best used to analyse longitudinal data is beyond the scope of this book. Below are some simple definitions of different commonly used statistical methods for analysing longitudinal and complex data, but these need to be determined by your research question.

Definitions of statistical analyses you might need

Mediation is determining whether one variable impacts another via its effect on a third.

Figure 5.1 An example of a mediation relationship

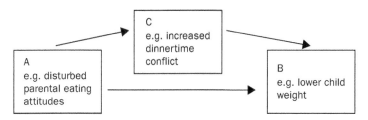

For example, Stein, Woolley, Cooper and Fairburn (1994), found that parents who had struggled with eating due to eating disorders had children who had a lower body weight. However, this was largely explained by dinner-time conflict, proposed to be caused by the stress of eating and food for these parents. Variable A, parental eating attitudes, did impact variable B, child weight, but this was mostly because variable A impacted variable C, dinnertime conflict, and variable C then impacted variable B. This is a mediation relationship.

Moderation happens where one variable influences the relationship between two others.

Figure 5.2 An example of a moderation relationship

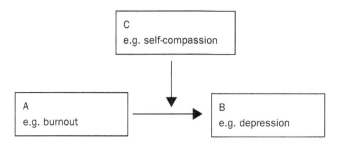

If a variable is a moderator, it changes how two other variables relate to each other. Kyeong (2013) explored the relationship between academic burnout and depression in Korean students. They found that there was a relationship between these two variables, but that for students with high levels of self-compassion the relationship between burnout and depression was non-significant, and yet for students with low levels of self-compassion it was highly significant. Thus, the level of self-compassion significantly moderated the relationship. As you can see, burnout (the independent variable) does not change self-compassion (the moderator), nor self-compassion change depression (the dependent variable), rather the level of the moderator changes the relationship between the other two variables. It is worth noting here that you can find a moderating relationship even when there is not a significant relationship between your two main variables as the moderator could make one relationship positive and one negative.

Structural Equation Modelling (SEM) is an umbrella term for a set of statistical techniques that aim to test the relationships between both latent and manifest variables.

Manifest variables are those that are tested directly, for example, height, weight, blood sugars, etc. Latent variables are those that are not measured directly but are implied by indirect measurement. For example, poverty might be measured by combining indices of household income, benefits, house-size, disposable income, etc. In psychology there are lots of variables that we measure in a way that can be considered direct but can also be considered indirect. We often measure depression using questionnaires that ask about lots of symptoms that can be attributed to depression, and we add the answers up to give a total score. Most of the time we treat this as a manifest variable and as a direct indication of the level of depression someone has. However, it is also possible to treat the individual answers to each question as contributing to a latent variable, using appropriate statistical analyses.

To find a latent variable, individual observations are subjected to a factor analysis (see below).

SEM combines manifest and latent variables in its analysis, which means it can account more fully for measurement error. Furthermore, it examines linear causal relationships between several variables simultaneously using path analysis, making it more powerful than simpler regression analyses.

Path Analysis is a technique for doing lots of regression analyses at once, accounting for all the others. The researcher specifies the paths to be tested, by developing a model that proposes particular directions of effect between specific variables, and then the analysis considers all these simultaneously. Often you need specialist software to do path analysis, and you also need a strong model to base your own model on.

Factor Analysis is one way of reducing a dataset into smaller numbers of variables. It looks for relationships between individual items/observations/ measurements and determines the best way of splitting up the data so that measurements within each variable are maximally related to each other. You can contrast it with cluster analysis that tries to cluster the participants based on their characteristics. Factor analysis tries to cluster individual items/observations/measurements together to make valid and reliable variables.

Partial Least Squares Modelling is a regression technique that takes a set of correlated predictors, and through examining how they are related to each other (analysis of the covariance) reduces them into a smaller number of predictors. This smaller set of predictors not only makes sense of a lot of inter-correlated predictors, but it can also be used more effectively in regression models. Because PLS tells you something about how the predictors are related to each other, as well as how they are related to the dependent variables, it is particularly suited to modelling. What makes PLS different to other kinds of dimension reduction techniques is that it takes into account how the independent and dependent variables are correlated.

A note on confounding variables: Confounding variables are those which influence our independent and dependent variables and/or the relationship between them and therefore can make our conclusions invalid. They are really important in experimental studies where you want to conclude that the manipulated variable did indeed cause the change in the dependent variable. However, when you are using large datasets, it is likely that you will not be viewing these variables as confounding but as important influences in the model – if they are important enough to change our conclusions, then in applied research we probably need to take them into account!

Philosophy

You are probably choosing to use this kind of data because you either want to look at lots of different variables at the same time or because you want a representative sample. This would usually speak to a realist perspective. An empiricist philosophy would make claims that the findings are true, whereas the critical realist philosophy would make claims that the data contribute to understanding the truth of the topic better.

What kind of questions are best answered using this method?

The best questions to ask using existing data are those that benefit from large numbers of participants or from good representative data. For example, you can only test a full model with lots of variables using large datasets, and while we always want good representative data, this can be crucially important when you are asking politically sensitive questions. For example, it is no good asking about the impact of poverty with a self-selected sample who have the time and resources to take part in your individual research study. In addition, with sufficient participants more complex questions can be answered, such as what happens to different kinds of people over time, and what influences these different trajectories.

Longitudinal research is very important to answer causal questions. Longitudinal studies do not answer causal questions as well as experimental designs, where the cause and effect are more closely linked due to having good control over the manipulation, but they are more effective than cross-sectional studies, where causality cannot be inferred at all (see O'Laughlin,

Martin & Ferrer, 2018 for discussion of the use of mediation analyses cross-sectionally and longitudinally). Longitudinal studies contribute to better understanding of directions of effect between different variables and these can sometimes challenge the assumptions of cross-sectional studies (see van Eijck, Branje, Hale & Meeus, 2012, for an example of this). More often, however, the relationship between variables is bi-directional, with each variable affecting the other over time. This may be very important to understand in terms of offering effective interventions or help and support for people.

The other kind of question that can be answered using these databases are ones in which having significant numbers of people from a minority group is important. This might be people with a minority medical diagnosis or genetic condition, or it might be people from a minority ethnic group or minority gender group. Trying to recruit minority groups in smaller studies often involves making practical decisions about how to recruit, all of which can lead to quite biased samples. If online support groups are used, then we inadvertently exclude those people who either do not wish for this kind of support and/or do not have internet access. If we go through services, we exclude those who do not access services; often an already marginalised group. If we advertise generally, we are likely to access those who are interested in the research question, and who have the capacity to remember to respond to a research advertisement, the ability to make the response, and the language and cognitive skills to understand our advertisement. Epidemiological studies aim to both sample a diverse sample, and to weight the data to take account of people in the community who are missing from the sample. Thus, when we explore the data from minority groups, we are likely to be minimising our biases in recruitment.

NB: Our samples are nearly always biased, but in order to recruit people from minority, marginalised or discriminated against groups, we often have to choose recruitment procedures that maximise numbers rather than reduce biases.

What are the key steps to using this method?

Find the question. There is a significant risk in using existing data that we go on a 'fishing expedition'. That is, we run lots of different analyses before we find one that is significant, perhaps unusual or surprising, and then go and write that up. This is bad practice and bad news for science (see Chapter 12 of Spiegelhalter, 2019). Therefore, if we are to use existing data, we need to have a clear and well-argued research question and/or hypothesis. Furthermore, given we are choosing to use existing data to maximise the variables we can include in our model, we need to have a good grasp of the literature. What are the key confounding variables? What are the key demographic factors that might impact our results? What are the key variables in our proposed model? Even with large numbers of participants it may not be possible to put everything in our model and therefore our analysis, but to do a good research study a thorough understanding of the literature and therefore a good research question with good, clear research hypotheses will be needed.

Find the data. In conjunction with finding the question, you need to find the data. You need to be able to answer the question you are developing with the data available, therefore it is worth checking out possible datasets for the kinds of variables they have prior to finalising your research question. If there aren't any datasets out there that answers your question, then you need to find a different question, or collect it yourself. How do you find the data? There are a few hosts of datasets that are searchable (see resources below). These can take hours and even days of your life, but they are a good start if you haven't identified a dataset yourself. It might be that you are aware of datasets from services you have worked in, or from national datasets that you or an academic partner may be aware of. Finally, if you have read the literature, you may be aware of datasets that are large and have multiple time-points that have been used in previous studies. They may not be publicly available, but sometimes they are, and a quick search will take you to a website where you can apply for the data.

Get hold of the data. Different datasets have different methods of getting hold of them. Some are freely downloadable and some you apply for. Some you have to pay for, whereas some you need a local sponsor for – that is someone who will take responsibility for the study and ensure the data is kept safe and used well. Releasing the data to you can take months, so if you are time-limited you need to make sure you apply for the data well in advance.

Match your variables to the data you have available. Even if you have pored over data dictionaries (a document produced by the research team of what measures were collected, with what tests, instruments or questionnaires, and how these are coded in the database), made sure that the variables you need are in the dataset, there is always a gap between the best way of measuring the variables you have in your model, and how they are measured in the dataset. With large datasets you may be able to create latent variables, using SEM or factor analysis, but for other variables you will have to make do with a measure that is good enough, rather than the one you would have chosen yourself. For example, you might be interested in depression, and the measure used is one of general wellbeing. If your key variable isn't measured well, you will have probably spotted that and will either choose a different question or a different dataset, but if it is a more minor variable in your model, you may make this compromise for the benefits of using existing and large datasets.

Create a usable dataset. Creating a usable dataset involves pruning the data by taking out variables you don't need and participants you don't want to include – basically removing the columns and rows that are not needed to answer your research question. This process might be iterative as you decide which variables are going to be included in your model and which aren't.

If you are using existing data that hasn't already been cleaned you will need to think about missing data and whether you are going to exclude participants because of missing data or whether you are going to impute your data to create a full dataset. If you are using a managed dataset then you need to think about how the data is weighted and how you are going to include weighting in your analysis.

Initial analyses and checking of assumptions. By now you will already have a good idea of how your data is behaving, but time spent getting to know your data is time well spent. What are the distributions of your variables? Are the means on your measures similar to other studies you have read? What are the relationships between your variables? Are they linear or non-linear, or is there no relationship? If you are working with longitudinal data what do the data do over time? It is worth checking out whether you have gender differences on your variables, or relationships with age, SES, ethnic background, even before you test your model. None of these investigations change your research question or your plan but understanding your data and the relationships between the variables will help with interpretation of more complex models. It is worth noting that this stage also helps you get confident with your statistics, and with using your statistics software.

Hypothesis testing. The final stage is to test your model. This stage can still go wrong. Your model might not resolve, it might be overfitted, or when all the variables are in the model some of the relationships might go in the opposite direction to the one predicted. However, if you have got to this stage, you will be able to ask interesting questions with great data and you will inevitably have something you can report.

How does this method usually go wrong and what can you do about it?

Things can go wrong at any of the stages above. It can happen that you know of a dataset that you can get access to within a reasonable timeframe and have a great idea for a research question, but that when you go to the data it doesn't have the right variables. Sometimes it looks like the data is available but then when you get the data there is too much missing data or the variables don't match well enough. Sometimes just getting hold of the data takes so long you have to change plan and then finally there can be difficulties aligning the research question with the measures taken of them, and the analyses that will test the hypotheses.

The main thing to do to overcome these difficulties is to plan well and to take your time. Take time with your reading and finding/developing your model to test. Take lots of time checking out possible databases and reading their data dictionaries carefully to determine what variables they have included and how they have measured them. Leave lots of time to get the data. Take lots of time getting your statistical skills up to scratch. Finally, take lots of time getting your data into a usable form. You should be able to give your datafile to someone else in your research team and for them to be able to answer your questions using your analysis plan with no extra work.

What are the practical issues associated with this method?

The practical issues are covered above, as there are no practical issues in collecting the data, only in getting the data.

Ethics

If you are using a widely available dataset, such as one of the key epidemiological datasets, then there are many ethical advantages. Participants will have consented for their data to be used for research studies. They will have been fully informed about how the data will be kept and used, and someone else will have anonymised the data. For datasets where combined data may identify individual participants there will be rules in place to ensure this doesn't happen. Furthermore, when the data is released, you will likely have to sign up to keeping the data safe.

There are additional wider ethical benefits of using these datasets. Participants' time is well used as so many questions can be answered using it. Furthermore, the questions that can be asked may be more meaningful and be closer to helping us determining what interventions might be useful.

If you are using existing datasets collected by a service some of the ethical advantages mentioned above may be present, particularly the advantages around the results being very meaningful. However, sometimes in busy services the process of getting consent for using the data is not as robust. Under GDPR, data can only be used either with consent or for public or legitimate interest, although sensitive, vulnerable health data should only be used with consent. It is worth working closely with the service to ensure that people have been giving consent for their data to be used for research purposes as well as clinical purposes.

Example: Developing a project using an existing dataset

O'Rourke, S. and Wilson, C. (2021). Contextual family factors in the relationship between paternal depression and child internalising. Paper presented at the 13th Annual Research Conference of the Growing up in Ireland National Longitudinal Study of Children.

See: https://scholar.google.com/citations?view_op=view_citation&hl=en&user=B29P_6IAAAAJ&cstart=20&pagesize=80&sortby=pubdate&citation_for_view=B29P_6IAAAAJ:iH-uZ7U-co4C

Stephen was completing a masters in applied psychology during the early phases of COVID-19. Collecting data was going to be tricky. A project was planned in a hospital, but with regulations about meeting people face-to-face changing all the time it wasn't possible to pursue it. Stephen and I were both interested in child and family issues, and we had been talking about parenting factors involved in children's difficulties, so when we decided to change direction we started thinking about the Growing up in Ireland (GUI) database. As we started talking about parenting in relation to children's emotional difficulties it became clear we were both interested in the unique role of fathers. So, we split the jobs. Stephen started looking at the data dictionary for the GUI database to see what variables were separated for fathers and mothers, while I started looking at the literature. There wasn't an available model, so we put together a model based on models of involvement of fathers in children's anxiety, involvement of fathers in children's wellbeing more generally, as well as models of involvement of mothers/parents in children's depression and wellbeing.

We then checked which variables in the theoretical model were present in the data. Some of them were measured really well, but others were only approximately measured. For example, there was a great measure of depression in fathers, but for children the measure we had access to measured internalising difficulties. However overall, we decided that all the variables we were really interested in were measured well enough.

Stephen didn't feel confident in learning lots of new complex statistical techniques in the time available, given that the programme he was enrolled on was time-limited, and we were already on his second planned project. Therefore, we discussed how to examine the models we developed given the statistical knowledge he already had. We used standard regression models and the total scores on the measures (meaning there was no need for factor analysis or finding latent variables) to look at relationships over time. Many psychological variables are very stable over time, and therefore most of the variance may be best accounted for by the stable characteristic of the person so we included child internalising problems as both a predictor variable (at time one), and a dependent variable (at time two). We wanted to show whether our other predictor variables had any additional predictive value on top of the stable characteristics of the children. Indeed father–child conflict and father parenting style both added to the prediction of later internalising difficulties in children in addition to the strong predictor of previous internalising difficulties.

Further reading

Baron, R. M., & Kenny, D. A. (1986) The moderator-mediator variable distinction in social psychological research: Conceptual, strategic, and statistical considerations. *Journal of Personality and Social Psychology*, 51, 1173–1182.
  The key paper for understanding statistical moderation and mediation.

Cumming, G. (2011) *Understanding the New Statistics: Effect sizes, confidence intervals and meta-analysis.* Abingdon: Routledge.
  This book sets out some key problems with null hypothesis significance testing and offers alternatives.

Hanna, D. & Dempster, M. (2012) *Psychology Statistics for Dummies*. Chichester: John Wiley & Sons.
It does what it says on the tin!

Pallant, J. (2020) *SPSS Survival Manual: A step-by-step guide to data analysis using IBM SPSS*, 7th edition. London: Routledge.
An essential guide for many students I have worked with.

Spigelhalter, D. (2019) *The Art of Statistics*. London: Pelican Books.
This is a very accessible book on what statistics can and can't do.

Tabachnick, B. G. & Fidell, L.S. (2012) *Using Multivariate Statistics*. Boston, MA: Pearson.
A guide to more complex statistics.

Websites that show you where to find data

https://www.icpsr.umich.edu/web/NACDA/search/studies?start=0&sort=TITLE_SORT%20asc&ARCHIVE=NACDA&rows=50
https://guides.library.ucla.edu/psychology/data
https://data.world/datasets/psychology

Websites of longitudinal studies

https://hrs.isr.umich.edu/about Health and retirement study
https://www.elsa-project.ac.uk/ English Longitudinal Study of Ageing
https://tilda.tcd.ie/ The Irish longitudinal study on ageing
http://www.bristol.ac.uk/alspac/ Avon longitudinal study of parents and children
https://www.growingup.ie/ Growing up in Ireland
https://growingupinaustralia.gov.au/ Growing up in Australia

Chapter references

Kyeong, L. W. (2013). Self-compassion as a moderator of the relationship between academic burn-out and psychological health in Korean cyber university students. *Personality and Individual Differences*, *54*(8), 899–902.

O'Laughlin, K. D., Martin, M. J., & Ferrer, E. (2018). Cross-Sectional Analysis of Longitudinal Mediation Processes. *Multivariate Behavioral Research*, *53*(3), 375–402. https://doi.org/10.1080/00273171.2018.1454822

Stein, A., Woolley, H., Cooper, S. D., & Fairburn, C. G. (1994). An Observational Study of Mothers with Eating Disorders and Their Infants. *Journal of Child Psychology and Psychiatry*, *35*(4), 733–748. https://doi.org/10.1111/j.1469-7610.1994.tb01218.x

van Eijck, F. E. A. M., Branje, S. J. T., Hale, W. W., & Meeus, W. H. J. (2012). Longitudinal Associations Between Perceived Parent-Adolescent Attachment Relationship Quality and Generalized Anxiety Disorder Symptoms in Adolescence. *Journal of Abnormal Child Psychology*, *40*(6), 871–883. https://doi.org/10.1007/s10802-012-9613-z

6 Designing experiments

Experiments have been the backbone of psychological research for many years. However, they are rarely used in applied psychological settings. This may be due to our reluctance to manipulate variables in people we work with, perhaps because we view them as vulnerable, or because in order to run a good experiment we often need to sacrifice ecological validity for internal reliability (more on this below). That means we often cannot look very directly at the phenomenon we are interested in, rather we have to look at it slightly sideways, perhaps by using a different population or perhaps by keeping lots of factors very controlled. Maybe these concessions mean that our experiment doesn't seem to answer a question close to the problem we want to work on. However, there are great advantages to running experiments: often our sample size calculation will show that we need fewer participants, we can isolate the precise thing we are interested in rather than look at a wide range of variables, and perhaps most importantly experimental design is the best design for looking at causality and directions of influence. In real life many relationships between variables are bi-directional, that is, each variable influences the other, and they are often both impacted by many other factors. However, by isolating one specific factor, keeping other factors stable (or controlling for them) and testing to see whether it affects another we can see whether changing it may have an impact on the outcomes.

What is this approach?

In true experimental design one factor is manipulated to have at least two conditions, and the effect on the outcome is measured. For example, you could manipulate mood so that some participants are made sad and some are made happy, or manipulate feedback on a task so some people think they have done well and some think they have done badly. However, some things aren't very easily manipulated and so a related type of design, a pseudo-experimental design, could be used. It may be difficult to manipulate your key variable something stable like a personality trait, such as optimism or extroversion, or something about the person, such as age or height. It may be unethical to manipulate a particular variable for example, if you wanted to explore how depression impacts cognition, it would be unethical to try and make people depressed for research purposes. In this case then, creating naturally occurring different groups and comparing outcomes across those groups might help you answer questions that could typically be answered using experimental design. This can be conceptualised as a between group differences design (see Chapter 7), but in a pseudo-experimental design, you are more likely to be interested in one particular group and the impact of the differences on a limited set of outcomes. It is likely to be driven by a hypothesis rather than a research question, and you will make efforts to keep all other variables between the groups the same.

Another variant on experimental design that should be mentioned here is using your participants as their own controls. Most experimental research chooses different groups for different manipulations, but it may be possible for your own participants to be their own control group (see example below for a within-participant experimental design). You may be able to manipulate mood in one direction and then the other. This kind of design comes with several complications (as explained later in this chapter section), but it also provides additional strength of interpretation and often reduces your required sample size further.

Philosophy

In experiments you often want to find an answer. Does manipulating mood change behaviour? Does manipulating behaviour change beliefs? It lends itself to null hypothesis significance testing based on strong hypothesis development and therefore has a more positivist epistemology than other kinds of applied psychological research. Most experiments do assume that if the manipulated variable has an impact on the outcome, then this is what happens in real life. However, using experiments in applied psychological settings often comes with caveats. Often the experiment sets up the manipulation so that it is simpler than real life. Often, we so carefully control additional variables that it isn't clear that this method applies to the full range of people we are working with. However, if we are taking a critical realist stance we should not take the outcome of one experiment as definitive. There are myriad studies in psychology's history that should be warnings to us (see Tim Harford's books, *How to Make the World Add Up* and *The Data Detective*). These are studies where a single finding has been seen as the truth, and then subsequent attempts at replication have not substantiated them (for example Amy Cuddy's seminal study on the power pose and how it increases your confidence; Carney et al. 2020, or John Bargh's early study on priming and its effect on how fast you walk down a corridor; Bargh et al. 1996). Many journals do not want to publish replications and many authors doubt themselves and think they have done the experiment wrong in some way if they don't replicate previous exciting findings. However, this leads to us trusting single experiments. A critical realist epistemology would find us searching out a variety of evidence to help us get at the truth, whether this might be experiments run by different labs, experiments run with different populations, especially those demonstrating cross-cultural stability of findings, or whether it might be searching out additional methodologies to help us best understand the results of one single experiment.

What kind of questions are best answered using this method?

The best kind of questions you can answer with experiments are of the kind 'does X effect/change Y?'. However, it might not always be obvious that you are actually interested in that as a question. If you are interested in whether your intervention works or not, then it might not be immediately clear that this is essentially a question of whether X (your intervention) effects Y (your outcome). It may be that you are interested in more nuanced questions such as 'in what circumstances does X effect Y?'. In this case, you may have a number of different conditions that differ across different dimensions.

What are the key steps to using this method?

Determine what you want to find out, i.e. what your research question is, and what your hypotheses are. Experimental design works very well to test theories. Often when we try and test a theory we look for how variables are associated with each other, or whether different groups of people are different, but experimental studies often explain how our variables influence each other, not just whether or not they are associated with each other.

From your research question and hypotheses you will start to **determine** *what* **you need to manipulate and** *how* **to manipulate it.** Some variables are commonly manipulated, such as mood, but others require more thought. For example, if you want to manipulate cognition, how do you get someone to think something or in some way that isn't their natural way of thinking? Your research team is vital here for repeated conversations about your question and what variable you can and need to manipulate.

Determine what you will measure as your outcome. You need to think about *what* you want to measure and *how* you will measure it. Sometimes what we want to measure can be impacted by how we measure it. For example, if you get people to rate their current mood, then reflecting on how they feel to answer the question can change their mood, which leads to the next step.

Determine the additional steps needed in your experimental design. If you are going to get participants to rate mood, can you get them to do this repeatedly so that they don't think too much about it at the crucial point, and therefore you minimise the impact of asking about it? How will you check if your manipulation has worked? If you have tried to manipulate things that are essentially internal to the person (mood, cognition, etc.), then you will have to ask them to report on this in order to determine whether the manipulation worked. Are you going to do this using open-ended questions, or Likert scales? Do you need multiple questions to verify it, or is one sufficient? Some experiments might need filler tasks and these need to be designed so they don't interfere with the task. This can be harder to design than you think! If you are interested in mood or cognition, you may find that most tasks impact mood or cognition! Colouring pages? What if the child has a physical coordination diffi-culty? Sorting task? Could be hard for some and easy for others, which impacts cognitive load. Experimental studies you have read, and your research team, are the resources you need to use to plan this.

Now you have your method more or less sorted, then you can start to **think about your participants**. If you are manipulating something that could increase distress or risk, then unless there is a very good reason to use vul-nerable participants, you are likely to choose a general population sample, rather than a clinical sample of participants. If you really want to focus on participants with certain kinds of difficulties, then you might want to design a pseudo-experiment that can capture natural differences rather than manipulat-ing variables. Of course, if your manipulation is designed to help a particular group, for example a psychotherapeutic intervention, then you are likely to want to check that it works for the people it is supposed to work for, and you will likely choose people who have certain kinds of difficulties. This is a good time to check out your *required sample size* (see Chapter 2 for sample size calculators) as that will also determine who your potential participants might be. Does your research question require you to have people of a certain age, or with certain kinds of experience (or lack thereof – e.g., people who haven't experienced trauma)? If not, can you be inclusive in your recruitment? Often experiments are kept tight to ensure that it is the manipulated variable that causes the differences, but if each group is similar then it is possible to keep the inclusion criteria wide. If you are doing a true experiment, then you finally need to work out *how you will randomise your participants*. There are some good online randomisation programmes that allow you to do full randomis-ation, block randomisation, and stratified randomisation. Full randomisation means that you randomise all your participants all at once. Block randomis-ation splits the full sample into blocks and randomises within these blocks as well as across the whole sample. The advantage of this is that you maintain a similar level in each of your experimental groups as the experiment progresses. This can minimise additional environmental effects on your experiment. In full randomisation you can, by chance, get most people in one group taking part in the middle of summer, with lovely weather, easy transport, holidays, and most people in the other group taking part in winter with cold wet days, transport strikes and no holidays planned. If your manipulation is powerful then these extraneous variables should not have much effect, but sometimes they can (or a global pandemic can interrupt recruitment) and so block randomisation might be helpful. Stratified randomisation is where different kinds of participants are grouped together prior to randomisation, for example you could stratify people by their age, and randomise younger and older participants separately. This can be helpful if you are recruiting a relatively small sample and the variables that you stratify by are potentially important to your outcome.

Now you have your overall design and your participants, you need to **con-sider more closely your procedure**. Questions that you can ask yourself as you plan your procedure are:

- What factors might influence the outcome as well as the manipulation and how can I minimise this? With a tight experimental procedure then this involves thinking about every detail.
- When will you ask your participants to consent and will the information you provide influence their response to the experimental manipulation?
- When will you ask your participants to complete any measures and how might this influence their responses?
- Where will the experiment take place and how will you ensure consistency across different places that you will carry out the experiment?
- What practising do you need to do with your participants to ensure that they have understood and can complete the experimental manipulation?
- How are you testing your outcome? Are you looking for change scores from pre- to post-manipulation and comparing differences in these changes, or are you just looking at changes after the intervention and will use pre-manipulation measures to determine pre-group differences?
- How are you going to test that your manipulation worked?
- Are you going to check what impact any filler tasks have had on your participants?
- When are you going to de-brief your participants in relation to your experimental manipulation and do you know what you will do if your participants are affected by the manipulation beyond what is expected?

In an intervention study you need to consider when participants will complete basic information about themselves, and when they will complete their outcomes measures. You need to think about the integrity of the intervention and whether all participants had a similar enough and good enough experience. This involves thinking about the people running the intervention, maybe performing formal integrity checks, and measuring things like how many sessions people attended and/or which tasks they completed. Ethics is discussed further below, but you also need to think about your control group carefully, as it is unlikely to be ethical to not offer your control group anything. If the control group is treatment as usual you need to think about how to document that in case it overlaps with your intervention, and if it is a waiting list, then you need to think about what support might be offered to participants while they are waiting.

Prior to running your actual experiment, you want to **pilot it.** In no other method described in this book is this more important. If you are running an intervention, then you are likely to have developed the intervention in your own practice prior to thinking you want to evaluate it, but if you are doing a single session manipulation it is highly worth piloting the procedure to check how it works and whether you need any changes prior to running the experiment itself.

Now you can recruit your participants and run your experiment! I am a fan of post-experiment debriefing, not only to check whether participants are OK, but also to check in with participants about their experience of the experiment. Sometimes, especially when you don't reject the null hypothesis – i.e., the experiment hasn't produced the predicted outcome – this debrief can tell you more than the experiment itself. This might not be something that you can write about in a journal article, but if you are writing up for an academic course, then you can certainly reflect on the process of the experiment.

Analysis and write up. Those simple words hide a world of complication and difficulty, but they are the last step in your study. What do you do if your manipulation didn't work? What if your practitioners didn't stick to the intervention manual? What if there was something else unintended that influenced your results? For example, one of the schools you recruited from only invited the 'best' students and another only invited the students who were causing problems in the classroom, or one consultant only invited patients with very severe difficulties to take part in the intervention and another only invited patients with very mild difficulties. Some of these are discussed below in what can go wrong, but it is worth giving yourself sufficient time for this stage of the research process.

How does this method usually go wrong and what can you do about it?

There are myriad ways in which experiments can go wrong. Some of these are due to poor planning, and some are beyond your control. However, both can lead to important learning and so should not be a reason not to do an experiment.

The main way in which experiments go wrong is that the manipulation doesn't work. Two things can really help with this – participant practice and piloting. This takes time but is worth it. Post-experimental debriefing can also throw light on what went wrong, and although not as good as getting your experiment to work, this can give you new directions for your research to go in and can increase your understanding of your topic.

In experimental research you want to make sure you are manipulating the construct you think you are. This is a conceptual issue and is best helped by talking to other experimentalists in your field who can help you think through the construct and how it might be possible to manipulate it. For example, there have been some interesting studies that have tried to manipulate intolerance of uncertainty. However, what they often manipulate is uncertainty itself, rather than the intolerance of it. This is fine and can make a good experiment, but these are conceptually different constructs and so need to be thought about and written about differently.

The other thing you need to think about is how the method of participant response might impact the outcome. There have been some interesting studies where the participant had to raise their hand or press a buzzer when a particular kind of thought entered their head. However, the process of raising a hand or pressing a buzzer can impact thought processes, particularly by interrupting them.

Another thing that can be tricky with experimental designs is recruiting sufficient participants. There are lots of reasons for recruiting sufficient participants:

you will likely power your study sufficiently leading to fewer type two errors (see Chapter 2); you will also be less likely to end up with chance significant differences between your groups on your confounding variables and you will also likely understand your topic better by being present for a wide variety of responses. If you are running the experiment yourself this can take a lot longer than simply giving participants some questionnaires to fill in. The time taken to run the experiment is taken away from time available to recruit participants. It might be that this isn't an issue for you if you are embedded in a practice or service and can recruit over time, but most research projects are time-limited and so having sufficient time to recruit participants and to run the experiment is crucial. It might be that there are people who are happy to help you with your study, for example running the experiment for you or alongside you, or it might be that you can choose a different approach, such as within-subject experimental design. There are some questions that a within-subject experimental design works very well for as you have two conditions rather than two groups. You might want to randomise your order of presenting the conditions to ensure you don't get a practice effect (where participants get better at something when they repeat it) or a saturation effect (where participants get worse at something when they are bored by it), but you may also keep the conditions in the same order to ensure everyone has the same experience of the experiment.

In an experiment you control as many confounding variables as you can, but collect data on those you can't. These data help you understand your findings, not to change your hypotheses or write up a different aspect of the experiment later. This might include capturing a description of the context of each experiment; we have done experiments in schools where the room set aside for our research is different each time. This might include collecting data on the service or practice context; we have recruited different participants from national specialist services when compared to local services for people with the same diagnosis. You almost certainly will collect good data on your participants as you will have to describe them in your write up, but this data is also useful for understanding unusual results!

Finally, one crucial thing that can go wrong in badly planned experiments is poor statistical planning. For example, in a recent experiment even when we thought we had worked out what we were going to analyse, when we came to it, we ended up with too much data that we couldn't collapse into total scores, and the data wasn't normally distributed, but there wasn't an obvious non-parametric statistical test that could be used. Part of this is solved by planning, but part of it is having someone with statistical expertise on your team.

What are the practical issues associated with this method?

You need to be prepared if you are going to run an experiment. This goes for online experiments where you need to have attention checks, extreme responding checks as well as expertise in putting complex experimental designs online, to physical experiments where you need to have your experimental procedure thoroughly planned, all your physical resources to hand and easy to use, as well as your inter-personal skills functioning at their best. Piloting your experiment really helps with this part of the process, and you can start by piloting on friends and family, even if they are not even close to the demographic of your participants! It is recommended to pilot on people who are potential participants prior to proper roll out of an experiment, but if the procedure is run exactly as you plan to do with your participants and no changes are needed, then it can be valid to use the data collected (NB: 'exactly as you plan' does include getting full informed consent).

There are additional practice considerations when trialling your intervention, but these are so numerous that instead of describing them all I would recommend checking out the further reading at the end of this chapter.

Ethics

In addition to the usual considerations of informed consent, anonymity, confidentiality and managing risk, managing your data well, and upholding participants' rights, experimental design leads to two key additional, and linked, ethical issues: deception and debriefing.

Deception. In some experiments you may not be able to be completely honest with your participants about the purpose of the experiment or the nature of the manipulation. For example, you might be interested in the impact of mood on attention processes. If you let your participants know that you are interested in what they are paying attention to, then this could impact *what* they pay attention to. Therefore, you might inform participants that you are interested in how it impacts their performance, and you might include both attentional tasks and other tasks. However, it is crucially important that participants are fully debriefed after the experiment. Having to tell your participants what the experiment is about should also ensure that you think very carefully about whether the deception is warranted. Low levels of deception, such as the example above about 'attention' vs. 'performance', should be easy to explain to participants – you are not correcting their understanding of the research they have taken part in, you are simply clarifying their understanding. However, if you are deceiving participants in a more serious way – perhaps persuading them of something that isn't true, for example by giving them false information about their abilities on a task – then you will have to explain to them that you deceived them. Some research is important enough that this is warranted, but lots of research isn't. If you keep your participants at the centre of your thinking, then you should be able to judge where the line is.

Deception might be different in other vulnerable groups. When we have not given children the full information about their participation, we have always given parents the full information. We ask them in the information sheet to not discuss the small details of the experiment with their children and we can check this out with the child at the start of the experiment (ask them – what do you think we are doing here today? What do you think I am going to ask you to do?), but it is important that parents or guardians give fully informed consent. If you think that if parents know what your experiment is about that they won't give consent, then maybe you need to think about whether it is a good idea.

Debriefing. As well as **debriefing** your participants when you have kept information about the study from them, we also need to think about other aspects of debriefing our participants. You may need to ensure that your participants do not continue to be impacted by the manipulation. That means they may need something to change their mood back to their usual levels. They may need corrective information about the scenario they were in to bring their beliefs back to their starting point, or you may want to take the opportunity to give new information about the topic of the experiment to help participants understand why you are doing the experiment and what they have just contributed to.

Example: Going from observation to experiment

Lynch, J. & Wilson, C. (2018). Exploring the impact of choral singing on mindfulness. *Psychology of Music*, 46(6), 848–861.

Julie came to me with a passion for choral singing. Not only was she a keen choral singer (as am I), but she had also read the literature round choral singing and its benefits. She wanted to do a study about the benefits but wondered how on earth she could go about this. Some of the benefits were physical and that didn't seem to fit with what she needed for her psychology project, such as improved breathing or heart rate regulation. Some of the benefits were social and those seemed hard to measure in the time available. However, there were many psychological benefits described. Some of the most interesting psychological benefits were those that were described in the qualitative studies. These included how singing kept you in the moment, how it grounded you, how it helped manage difficult feelings without any effort to resolve them or push them away. As Julie told me about the benefits these qualitative studies showed, I could not help think of the reported benefits of mindfulness. Julie wasn't interested in doing another qualitative study – she wanted to show the benefits rather than describe them, so we knew we wanted to plan a quantitative study. I sent her away to read about mindfulness and she came back understanding why I had made the link. We decided that the study would be an experimental study of whether choral singing improves state mindfulness.

That was a very good start. We had gone from the observation to a question, but now the difficult part started – what could we actually do? If the study was to show that choral singing increased state mindfulness, we would definitely have to measure state mindfulness before and after choral singing. It didn't quite make sense to make new people start choral singing, just as it didn't make sense to compare those who did to those who didn't. So, we started with the idea that we would measure state mindfulness before a choral rehearsal, and then after it and see if it changes. That was major hurdle number one – there wasn't a measure of state mindfulness that we were happy with. Most measures measured trait mindfulness (trait is about a characteristic of the person, whereas state is the current emotional level). Julie set about changing the wording of the measure that most fit the kind of mindfulness we thought we wanted to measure (i.e., the one that had most face validity for us and our study), from general statements to present moment statements and we used our data to validate our version of the questionnaire.

The second set of conversations and decisions were about the experiment itself. We could have simply tested participants on our new measure before and after their rehearsal, but then we couldn't work out whether this was due to the rehearsal and the singing itself or whether it was due to something else, like the beauty of the music, the social connection, it simply being evening time, or something else – some choirs have very good tea and cake at their break times! We discussed these alternatives and decided based on a combination of theoretical knowledge, our own experience, and the pragmatics of running an experiment, that we would compare choral singing to listening to beautiful choral music. We felt that this was something we had control over as we could ask participants to take a few minutes to listen to a piece of music (we chose the music ourselves rather than let our participants choose, again to increase the internal validity by keeping the procedure standard). We could standardise the music by giving it out ourselves, thus increasing the internal validity of the experiment, and although we were also removing the social aspect of choral singing, we were controlling for something else that was known to effect mood positively. Our final decision to be made was around the kind of experiment. One option was to collect two groups – one who listened to music and one who attended a choral rehearsal. The other was to collect one group of people and get them to do both. The power of this second option was that it reduced the sample size and minimised the potential confounding variables that could occur between the two groups. We decided to do a within participant experiment where every person would both listen to music and would attend a choral rehearsal. The main disadvantages of this were that we were asking more of our participants, and that they would complete the measure four times. As it was a state measure (a measure of current state of mindfulness rather than a stable personality characteristic) we hoped that there wouldn't be learning effects (where someone gets 'good' at answering because they get to do it several times). Finally, we decided, mainly for practical reasons, that we would get everyone to complete the procedure in the same order – the rehearsal first and listening to music second. It might have been better to randomise the order to check that one didn't influence the other, but we thought that as our participants attended regular choral rehearsals if there was an effect of the first part of the experiment, namely the rehearsal, then this would be an effect anyway.

Further reading

Books

Miles, J. E., & Gilbert, P. E. (2005) *A Handbook of Research Methods for Clinical and Health Psychology*. Oxford: Oxford University Press.
A classic book with lots of good advice that is just as relevant nearly 20 years on.

Kazdin, A. (2021) *Research design in clinical psychology*, 5th ed. Cambridge: Cambridge University Press.
A giant in the field and a great overview of lots of different kinds of designs, but with great chapters including experimental design.

Harford, T. (2022) *The Data Detective: Ten easy rules to make sense of statistics*. London: Bridge Street Press.
An accessible book that should be required reading for anyone working with statistics.

Chapter references

Bargh, J. A., Chen, M., & Burrows, L. (1996). Automaticity of social behavior: Direct effects of trait construct and stereotype activation on action. *Journal of Personality and Social Psychology*, 71(2), 230.

Carney, D. R., Cuddy, A. J. C., & Yap, A. J. (2010) Power Posing: Brief nonverbal displays affect neuroendocrine levels and risk tolerance. *Psychological Science*, *21*(10), 1363–1368. DOI: https://doi.org/10.1177/0956797610383437

Harford, T. (2020) *How to Make the World Add Up: Ten rules for thinking differently about numbers*. London: Hachette.

7 Single case (experimental) design

Many practitioners work with one person at a time, whether this might be for therapy, or an assessment of their needs, or in supervision. We often notice unique things about the person in front of us, while also often noticing things they may have in common with others. We might notice that some things seem to work well, and others don't, and we might be curious about what it was that made the difference, or what the active ingredient is. It is perhaps this feature of some kinds of practical work that explain why single case approaches to understanding people have had a very long history. Sometimes this might be a detailed description of an individual's difficulties, a detailed description of the work or the therapy, or a detailed description of the person's neurological difficulties. However, there is also a rich history of single case design where discreet aspects of an intervention are tested to see if they do change outcomes in carefully controlled circumstances. Single case designs such as case series have also been used in the initial stages of developing a new intervention. Single case design is well suited to practitioners as it utilises their everyday work to produce research knowledge.

What is this approach?

Single case research design is where there is either a systematic description of an aspect of someone's presentation (case study) or an experiment where a single person is subject to different carefully controlled circumstances to see what factors have what effects on them (single case experimental research). The focus of this chapter is on the second of these, although there will be reference to the first. Single case experimental research involves multiple measurements of the outcome variable over time in response to either repeated manipulations, or different manipulations. For example, we could try and work out what kind of visual stimulus a baby prefers by alternating access to a red rattle and a blue rattle several times and seeing how many times they look at and reach for each. Alternatively, we could try and work out the triggers for withdrawing behaviours in someone with an intellectual disability by alternating everyday noise and complete quiet.

Single case experiments have historically been analysed visually, exploring the measured outcome after each stimulus or manipulation is made and visually inspecting the graph produced to look at the patterns of change. This is still important in single case experimental design and especially in some fields such as Applied Behavior Analysis (ABA) that focuses on observable behaviours as outcomes. However, more recently there has been a focus on statistical analysis of single case data in addition to visual inspection. Non-parametric approaches can prove very helpful to test particular hypotheses about our data such as trends in the mean values of the outcome in different phases of the experiment, or trends in the variability in the mean values of the outcome in different phases of the experiment. There are also statistical approaches to exploring individual data where there aren't multiple measurements, for example in simple pre–post designs for testing whole interventions, allowing both visual and statistical evaluation of the impact of therapy on individuals or small groups of individuals.

Philosophy

The central tenet of single case design is that it is idiographic. It focuses on the individual, rather than on average group differences, preferring an understanding of individual differences to an understanding of group differences in general. Single case design has a strong realist philosophy as it focuses on behaviours that are relevant to the individual or individuals in question. It rarely aims to further develop theory or general understanding and prioritises external validity and the applicability of the findings to the real world of the participant. Single case experimental design is empirical and often positivist as it is interested in cause and effect based on observations of behaviours in different circumstances, whereas case studies can be positivist, especially some of the neurological case studies, or interpretivist/constructionist, especially some of the early psycho-analytic case studies.

What kind of questions are best answered using this method?

For single case non-experimental design, the narrative case study provides an insight into unique features of people's lives. It maybe has more parallels with qualitative research, providing context and a rich description. However, by including some quantitative measures, and perhaps some single case analysis, such as analysis of reliable change and clinically significant change, the single case non-experimental study can be used readily in practice. It indicates whether your intervention works for the participants in your service. It can be viewed as part of an audit cycle, collecting data to see if your service impacts outcomes in the way you think it should. It can be viewed as a simple experimental design with pre and post measures allowing checking for change. It isn't highly controlled, there are lots of other factors that could have led to change, and therefore it is best suited for research questions that are specific to particular places, people or contexts.

As mentioned above, the single case experimental design has been widely used in ABA and other behavioural contexts, and so the questions that have tended to be asked are around specific interventions that impact on specific behaviours. It is focused on determining causality, like other experimental designs, and therefore the questions that are likely to be best answered using this approach are questions about processes and mechanisms.

What are the key steps to using this method?

Determine what outcome you are interested in. This is often an observable behaviour, but it could also be affect/mood, a score on a test or measure, or a self-report of an internal event such as experiencing a particular thought or image. If you are testing a novel intervention, then there might be outcomes you can track over time in addition to formal measures taken before and after the intervention, such as mood states or time spent in certain activities between sessions. These can complement outcome measures in interpreting the data.

Work out what kind of single case experimental design might help you answer your question. There are a variety of different designs, each of which has advantages and disadvantages. Things that can help you decide which approach might work best for you include:

Is your intervention reversible? If your intervention is reversible, for example putting someone in a noisy environment and then taking them out of that environment, then an ABAB or reverse design might work well, as might alternating treatment designs (the alternative treatment in this example being an unusually quiet environment). However, if your intervention is designed to teach someone skills or is in some other way irreversible, for example, by influencing their beliefs about something, then a simple AB design might work, as might a multiple baseline design.

Are you working on several different outcomes or just one? If you are aiming to change several different outcomes, then a within participant multiple baseline approach might work well. For example, if you want to see if noisiness is context dependent to eating behaviour, or whether it affects all kinds of behaviour, then you can test the impact of a quiet vs a noisy environment firstly on eating behaviour, but then on self-care task behaviours such as teeth cleaning, and then maybe on social behaviours such as interacting with others.

Have you time to get a stable baseline measure? If you can do lots of observations or measurements, or your measured outcome does not fluctuate very much then you may have chance to get a stable baseline, that is, make observations until the variance in measurements is predictable. If a behaviour is unpredictable, then this can take a very long time and lots of observations. Therefore, if the measured outcome has a rather fluctuating course, you may not be able to get sufficient baseline measures to get a stable baseline and a different design might be best.

Have you got several people lined up for the same intervention or experimental manipulation? If you already know that you have several people lined up to take part in your study, then a between-subjects multiple baseline design might be best. Here, you get to start the interventions with your participants at different times in their baseline measurement to ensure that it is the intervention itself that makes the difference, not something else.

Once you have a suitable design and your outcome decided, you need to **determine exactly what it is that you are going to do**. The key factor to good single case research is holding as much as you can stable so that you can be sure that it is your intervention or experimental manipulation that makes the difference. This involves thinking carefully about measuring outcomes (see more below) to ensure they are reliable and valid. It involves thinking carefully about who is doing the intervention in what context, with what instructions and with what timing. In between-groups designs or in larger experiments you try to ensure that there aren't factors that cause group differences by using a control group and/or by using large enough samples. In single case research these factors cannot be controlled for using these methods and therefore must be kept as stable as possible.

Just as you would for an experimental research design, it can be worth **piloting your intervention** to check that the instructions and the manipulation works. Running a single case experimental design or an experimental case series feels quite different to running other studies. Unlike other studies where recruiting participants is crucial and therefore a lot of energy is put into this aspect of the study, in single case research the crucial aspect is carrying out the intervention and collecting the data very carefully. Each experimental procedure may take days, carefully collecting data each day, maybe exactly at the same time every day. It may involve collecting data every week for months. As you have a single participant or a very small number of participants, it is important that no data collection is missed or done carelessly. While you are running your experiment you may decide that you want further participants, or you want further manipulations. Running a single case experiment is therefore an active process which needs to be planned for.

The final stage before writing up your experiment is to **analyse your data**. As analysis is special to single case designs; it is worth planning this prior to starting the experiment. It may be that you have training in ABA or another behavioural approach and simple visual inspection will be sufficient for you to be able to answer your research question. This might be especially true if you are doing single case experiments as a standard part of your practice rather than for wider research purposes. It might also be true if you can carefully control your experiment and ensure you have got a stable baseline and clear distinctions between the intervention and the alternative. The first step is to present your data clearly. This might involve various decisions about what data to present. Have you got raw scores that make sense to present as raw scores, or do you have to compute mean scores per day? Have you several different measurements for an outcome and, if you have, how are you going to combine these? There are good guides for clear presentation of data (see further reading below) which highlight both what an overall graph needs to include, but also how to represent different aspects of your data that tests your question. For example, you might only be interested in whether the average score changes between two phases, in which case you might graph the mean for each phase. You might be interested in an overall trend, in which case a fitted straight line is what you are looking for. You might be looking for variability in different phases or overlap between scores in different phases. These are all determined by your research question and can help you identify what to plot and how to represent it.

If you have several participants, it is often most helpful to present each person's data individually. Single case research is closest to an idiographic approach and representing participants individually allows the reader to judge the impact of the intervention, not only over time, but between individuals. If you want to go beyond visual inspection, then there are statistical techniques that can deal with data produced by single case experiments. You might need to seek specialist advice on these, as they aren't covered in most statistics books. However, they are well covered in books on using single case designs (see Further reading for this chapter). Your statistics for single case experiments, just as other statistics are, are driven by your hypotheses. Morley and Adams (1989) proposed that you might have one of several hypotheses:

1   The null hypothesis is that the series is random
2   That the series contains cyclical variation
3   That there is a trend in the mean of the series
4   That there is a trend in the variability of the series (Morley & Adams, 1989: p2)

Simple non-parametric statistics can help determine each of these (as discussed in both Morley and Adams, 1989, 1991, but also in Morley, 2018), but there are also newer techniques that centre around regression and randomisation tests. Planning your statistical analysis as a part of your research planning phase, rather than collecting data and then working out what to do with it, can ensure that there is a test that you can use when you have done all the hard work of collecting your data.

How does this method usually go wrong and what can you do about it?

The main thing that seems to go wrong in single case design is losing data. Because you often need multiple datapoints in order to determine whether it is your intervention or manipulation that made the actual difference, then it is quite easy to lose data. In other research designs if you lose data you recruit another participant. In single case designs, losing data makes so much more difference, as you may have days and days or even weeks of data from a single participant and collecting data from a different participant involves finding a participant who is similar enough to collect data from, and starting from the beginning. In the kinds of studies that use single case experimental design, neither of these are easy.

There are obvious things that you can do to minimise this occurrence. For example, developing good relationships with your service gatekeepers and your participants will ensure that they do their best to keep going with your procedure. You can set clear expectations at the start of the process about what will be happening, when, how, and for how long. You can try and plan a procedure that is as minimally invasive as possible for the participant(s), even if it leads to more work for you as the researcher. However, even with the best plans and the best relationships things can go wrong. So, what else can you do? If you have some knowledge about the service you want to recruit participants from, then you may be able to plan a design that allows for some missing data. For example, if you are aiming for a stable baseline, it might be OK that this isn't done by getting daily data. In general, the weaker the design, the more controlled the rest of the variables need to be, therefore if you know that your participant(s) sometimes doesn't attend the service where you are collecting data, it might be better to plan an ABAB design rather than a simple AB design.

What are the practical issues associated with this method?

There can be a lot of practical issues associated with this method. Collecting data very regularly, for example daily, is associated with a lot of practical issues, such as travel to your participant(s), trying to see them at a similar time each day or each week and fitting this round their schedule and yours, and little tolerance for you or them being sick, not feeling like doing the procedure, or having other things come up in your life. Even with looser single case narrative designs ensuring that you have permissions to contact participants at the end of interventions, even when they did not complete it, can take time and thought. If you are working in a busy service, you may not feel inclined to get data from people who dropped out of an intervention either because you feel you are being intrusive to them, or because you want to concentrate on the people who you are still working with. When you must keep gathering data in order to answer the research question, this can add extra strain!

There are additional practical issues associated with the repeated nature of this approach. No matter how hard we work to choose appropriate outcome measures, there may be unexpected practice effects as our participants complete questions repeatedly. There may be fatigue or disengagement. There may also be withdrawing of consent, either explicitly, or implicitly during the procedure.

Ethics

Although there are few additional ethical considerations for this approach per se, the kinds of studies that typically use this approach do require us to think carefully about ethics.

In terms of single case narrative approaches, it can be very easy to slip into thinking that it is just standard clinical practice, and you are just sharing practice. However, you are likely to be sharing personal and sensitive aspects of your participant's/client's life and therefore you need full informed consent. NB: if you are using this approach for research purposes – to disseminate widely through publication, talks or social media (see Chapter 16) – then you need a different kind of consent to the consent you need to share client information with your practice coordinators, educators and supervisors. This latter kind of sharing also requires explicit consent in most cases, but it is not usually reviewed and approved by an ethics committee. If you are a student needing to write up practice reports, speak to your educators and practice coordinators about what kind of consent you need for these.

In terms of single case experimental approaches, these have historically been very well utilised with people with intellectual disabilities, challenging behaviour, and other neurological disabilities. These groups could need support to give informed consent. For some, giving informed consent will not be possible. It is imperative that we provide sufficient support for people to give consent where they can, give assent where they can't, and to help others who may be asked for permission on their behalf to understand what the participant will be undertaking and what impact it might have. Some behavioural approaches can cause harm, and have done so historically, and so a true understanding of what the intervention is, what benefit it is intended to confer to the participant, and any risks of the intervention is paramount.

Further reading

Books

Kazdin, A. E. (2011) *Single-case research designs: Methods for clinical and applied settings*, 2nd edition. Oxford: Oxford University Press.
Kazdin has been writing about research design for a long time. He truly understands applied research and this book shows this.

Morley, S. (2018) *Single-case methods in clinical psychology: A practical guide*. Oxford: Routledge.
Although designed for clinical psychology, the principles and ideas in here are applicable to many settings.

Todman, J. B. and Dugard, P. (2001) *Single-case and small-n experimental designs: A practical guide to randomisation tests*. New York: Routledge.
A specific, but important, aspect of single case design, and very accessible.

Chapter references

Morley, S., & Adams, M. (1989). Some simple statistical tests for exploring single case time series data. *British Journal of Clinical Psychology*, 28(1), 1–18.
Morley, S., & Adams, M. (1991). Graphical analysis of single case time series data. *British Journal of Clinical Psychology*, 30(2), 97–115.

8 Between groups design

We all differ. Some of us are tall, some are short. Some people like blue, others prefer red. Some people take lots of risks, others try not to take any risks at all. Quite a lot of research involves identifying whether perceived group differences on key variables are genuine. Psychologically speaking, it makes sense to determine whether secondary school children are better at certain cognitive tasks than primary school children. We might want to know whether people with certain physical health conditions are more likely to have mental health difficulties. It might be helpful for us to know whether older adults have different attitudes towards technology when compared to younger adults. We have a human tendency to classify people into categories and therefore a human tendency in research to try and look for relevant group differences. When we use a between groups design, we choose groups relevant to our research question and test whether our outcome variable(s) differs between those groups.

What is this approach?

Between groups design is perhaps one of the simplest research designs there is. Many of the statistics we learned as an undergraduate, t-tests, ANOVAs, support our analysis. We only need to choose our outcome variables and how to measure them, and then to determine inclusion and exclusion in our groups. The rest is straightforward.

Philosophy

Our aim in comparing two groups is mainly to determine true differences in groups. We use our inferential statistics to try and show that the differences are not likely to be due to chance. Therefore, our epistemology is likely to be empiricist. We are making claims about the truth of the differences we observe. It is possible to compare groups in qualitative research, and the claims we make about the truths of any differences we find might be different. However, for most of our between-groups research we are taking a quantitative approach.

What kind of questions are best answered using this method?

The only kind of questions that can be answered using this method are those in which we are interested in group differences. The key to asking good questions using this method is to work out whether the differences we are interested in are meaningful and will truly help us answer our research question. I often see people wanting to research whether a certain group has higher levels of mental health difficulties or more sleep problems or greater cognitive deficits compared to another group. When you ask why, it is usually because they want to justify a level of service provision that is greater than for the general community. If service commissioners do want to see these numbers in order to ensure good service provision, then this is a good question to ask. It might be seen as theory-free research (see Chapter 3) and so guidelines about quality for this kind of research should be considered. However, more often than not these kinds of numbers do not lead to any additional service, and an audit of service provision and/or waiting lists might be a better use of time.

Alternatively, the research question might be driven by theory, and finding group differences might be crucial in determining the value of the theory. However, psychology and other social sciences have a history of finding group differences that have been used to further discriminate against a minority group. Choosing your theory wisely and involving your potential participants in the development of the research question can help overcome this, as can working closely with a diverse research team who are willing to challenge each other.

What are the key steps to using this method?

There are two main steps involved in using this method: choosing your participants and a suitable control group or groups; and choosing measures to compare them on.

Choosing your participants and control group(s)

Chapter 2 outlines some crucial considerations when determining your inclusion and exclusion criteria, and these are paramount when comparing groups. If you want to test whether there are genuine differences between two or more groups, then you need to make sure that there are no confounding factors that could account for those differences. This is one method where you might need strict exclusion criteria, so that you have true differences between your groups. For example, when researchers test differences between people who are depressed and people who aren't they often have an exclusion criterion that the group that is not depressed should never have had depression. They may also choose to include a second comparison group of people who have previously been depressed but are not currently depressed. When functional abilities are tested in children with learning or intellectual disabilities, there are often two control groups: one that is matched on overall cognitive ability or IQ, and one that is matched on chronological age. In health populations, you might choose a healthy control group as well as a group with a different health condition to the one you are interested in.

When you are comparing groups you do need to determine that the group differences aren't due to additional demographic factors and so you need to think about your recruitment strategy to ensure that your groups do not significantly differ on age, gender, SES, ethnicity, or other important characteristics. If you recruit a population of people with a health condition from a hospital but then compare them to undergraduate students, they are likely to differ on lots of different characteristics. If this is unavoidable then you can control for some of these statistically, but recruiting the correct control groups in the first place is better. One aspect of this is to determine from the literature what factors might be important to control for. The second is to make sure you are collecting sufficient information about your participants so that you can determine whether there are additional differences between the groups and, if necessary, control for these.

There are some strategies that can be used to match samples, including asking participants to nominate a friend who might be willing to take part, as this person is likely to share more key characteristics than someone from the general population. Another strategy is to over-sample the control group so that a sub-group of this can be used. You could either ask the control group to complete the full procedure, or ask them to complete screening measures and only invite some to complete the full procedure. You are likely to lose some participants in this two-stage process, but it does minimise the burden on participants, especially when it is possible their data will not be used in the final study.

Choosing your measures and procedures

Just as choosing your participants and control group or groups is crucial, when you are testing group differences you need to ensure you are measuring the right variables. Go back to your research question and your motivation for your research question. Are you sure you are interested in distress, anxiety or depression, or are you really interested in resilience or coping strategies? If you are interested in distress, are you interested in overall distress levels or are you interested in the percentage or proportion of people who have a clinical level of distress?

Once you are clear on what you are interested in measuring, you need to source measures that really measure it! You might not have much choice if there isn't funding for your study. You might need to choose measures that are freely available, and for some constructs you won't have much choice. At the very least you need to check that your measures have good psychometric properties. If you have a choice, then look at the psychometric properties of the measures, how widely they have been used, and the face validity of your measure, that is, how well you think it captures the construct that you are interested in.

Sourcing measures

How do you go about finding measures in the first place? It might be that you have access to a specific searchable database, such as APA's PsychTests. This can be a good place to start, both to get a sense of how many options you might have for your constructs, but also to see what kinds of measures are freely available.

You might have access to the test itself through your own practice, and so you can use Google Scholar or use a formal search engine to look for studies of the psychometric properties of the measure. Some regularly used measures in practice have excellent psychometric properties, but others have either untested psychometric properties, or poor psychometric properties. They might be useful in our practice, but they might not be good enough for research, where we need our measures to be comparable across different participants, across time, and we need them to measure the thing they say they do.

You can find measures through other people's research. Start by using a search engine to search for the construct in conjunction with the words measure and/or questionnaire, and/or survey. Google Scholar is a good place to start because it captures the most relevant articles first. It is also a good place to start because you can put full sentences into the search without significantly impacting the findings. For example, if you put 'measures or questionnaires on mentalisation' into PsychInfo then it will search for these words separately (there are ways of searching that don't separate them, but that adds a layer of complication), whereas in Google Scholar it will focus on articles that best match the full sentence. The results you might get from these searches are either individual measures that you can look at further, or if you are lucky, a review of different measures. What you are aiming to do with these initial studies is to identify several measures that might be appropriate for your own study. Once you have identified possible measures you need to find physical or electronic copies of these measures and identify psychometric studies of the measures. You need to be able to identify physical or electronic copies of the measure in order to determine whether you need to pay for it, whether there are copies available or whether it is just a research paper with a list of questions and a description of how to answer each question. You need to determine how your measures are scored and whether there is reverse scoring (this is where most questions indicate one valence of answer, for example, high scores are good, but some questions indicate the opposite valence, i.e., high scores are bad), whether there are sub-scales and whether you are recommended to use a total score or not. Finding the questionnaires themselves involves some detective work. You can search for them using a general search. This is often good at turning up measures that you must pay for, as you turn up websites where the measures are for sale. It is also good for turning up questionnaires that are freely available and that have their own website with all this information on it. In my experience, these two options are the least common. The most common experience is that you can't find a physical or electronic copy of the measure. You may need therefore to contact the original author, or, if the measure is old and the author has retired or moved on, contact the author of a paper that has used it recently. In recent papers authors' email addresses are part of their contact details, but for older papers you might have to search for the author and find their institutional affiliation. Most authors are quite happy to be contacted, although some will not have to time to get back to you or will have moved on and/or will not respond to emails. The final option is to recreate the measure from the information in the paper. I would only do this after you have exhausted all your other options, as it suggests that the measure isn't widely used, it might not have been appropriately validated, and it might not have the best psychometric properties. However, if the option you have is to recreate a measure, rather than create your own, that still might be a better option for you. NB: some measures are available in books or as appendices in papers. It is polite to request permission to use the measure from the author. Some authors of measures have forms to complete so that they can keep track of who is using their measures, whereas others are more informal. This step also ensures that you are not using a measure that you do need to pay for without paying for it.

Alongside the searches for the physical/electronic copies of the measures you can start to gather the psychometric data you need to evaluate the possible measures. These might be in specific studies of the psychometric properties or sometimes they are hidden within the early studies that are using the measure. This is more common when the measure was developed for a particular purpose and so there isn't a full paper describing the psychometric properties of it. It is always worth going back to the first citation of the measure. This should have some psychometric properties reported. You can then use forward citations to explore other psychometric studies of it. This is where your formal search engines are most useful. You can put the title of the measure into your search engine, with any combination of 'psychometric', 'reliability' and 'validity', and all the studies that have looked at the psychometric properties of your measure should be produced. Doing this in Google Scholar doesn't work because of its algorithms – you choose your search engine depending on what you need to search for! For some measures there will be many different studies of their psychometric properties, and you don't need to review them all. If you have the choice, look for large studies with good attention to the participants (those who didn't use just undergraduate students), good attention to different kinds of reliability and validity, and that match most closely the participants you want to recruit.

If you now have a list of possible measures and their psychometric properties, it is time to decide which to use. In the end it is down to you to decide but the factors you might want to take into account are the burden on participants both in terms of numbers of items, but also the language used in the measure, the face validity of the measure for your purpose, and finally, the structure of the measure in terms of sub-scales and total scores. This final one is important in determining your statistical plan, and therefore your planned sample size.

You might choose to create your own measure if there isn't one that truly captures what you need. This has advantages and disadvantages. The advantage is that you can capture exactly what you want by designing the questions yourself. The disadvantage is that you will have to measure the psychometric properties of your measure yourself. This can require large participant numbers. Some aspects of testing psychometrics require large numbers (factor analysis) or repeated administration of the measure (test–retest reliability). Many people simply report internal consistency, perhaps with some external test of face validity and for some studies this might be sufficient. However, if you do want to test group differences properly you not only need groups that are very separate from each other, you also need good measures.

Additional considerations

Getting the correct participants and measures is the key to good between-groups studies, however, there are a few additional considerations to be thought about.

Timing and organisation of collecting data

It might be a minor consideration, but if you collect all the data from your main group during summer and all the data from your control group in winter you are adding some additional potential confounds, and unlike demographic factors, this is hard to control for. This is also true if you collect all the data from your main group in person but collect all the data from your control group online. Sometimes we choose these options by accident, but ideally, we should think about these factors prior to starting our study.

Planning the statistical analysis

In between groups design research we may have to control for demographic variables statistically, and so we need to consider this at the start of the study to ensure we have sufficient participants. It is also worth thinking about how many variables we are comparing and whether we need to recruit enough participants to make multiple comparisons. This doesn't just happen when we ask participants to complete several questionnaires, but also when we have questionnaires with sub-scales and we want to compare the groups on each of the sub-scales. There are a number of statistical ways of making these multiple comparisons, from using MANOVA or MANCOVA, or adjusting our significant p value using a correction like Bonferroni, but we need to plan for these at the start.

A note on comparing groups in qualitative studies

It isn't all that common to compare groups in qualitative studies. This might be due to the approaches that are commonly used. It doesn't make sense in grounded theory as you want your theory to be as inclusive as possible (see Chapter 13). It also doesn't make sense in IPA, as this is an idiographic approach (see Chapter 14) and your aim is to elucidate the phenomenology of something. However, it is possible to compare groups qualitatively. Within an IPA methodology this basically involves doing two IPA studies, one on each of your groups, and then making some observations about key similarities and differences. It is possible, however, to use more flexible methods to look at group differences in qualitative studies. Thematic analysis, both in its non-interpretative form, and in its reflexive form, can be used to compare groups in qualitative research. Using a non-interpretative approach would involve developing the codes, and perhaps a codebook, and then looking to see whether there are differences between the groups in which codes are endorsed by each group. This is akin to making your qualitative data quantitative. Using this approach, you can either use the whole dataset to create your codes, or you can split the groups and develop codes in each group, and then go looking for the codes in the other group. Template or framework analysis might be an appropriate similar approach for this kind of analysis. Using a reflexive approach to compare groups is likely to be quite different. In this approach the whole dataset should be analysed without any consideration of which group a participant is in. The themes and the narrative of the data should reflect the whole dataset. All the coding and the development of the themes should be done for all the data first, and only at write up should the groups be considered. This ensures that the most relevant themes are included but that group membership is also considered. See Lindsay (2019) for further ideas on comparing groups in qualitative research.

How does this method usually go wrong and what can you do about it?

This method usually goes wrong when there is a characteristic of your participants that you haven't considered that potentially accounts for the differences between your participants. For example, you might be testing gender differences in a school population, and just by chance your female participants are, on average, younger than your male participants, and worse than that – age correlates with your main measure. You might be able to control for age in your analysis, but you might then not have the power to find any true group differences. This suggests a second key thing that goes wrong, and that is recruiting too small a sample size. If we haven't made a statistical plan, then we may fall into the trap of calculating a sample size based on a single analysis, for example, group differences in the total score on one of our measures. If we then want to explore group differences in the sub-scales of our measure, we may be underpowered. I've seen many a researcher appeal to individual hypotheses about each sub-scale in order to not make any corrections to the chosen significance level (p-value), but this is a false economy. You should not need statistical significance to publish a well-designed, well carried out study, and therefore massaging your statistics to ensure you can report some significant results at an arbitrary value of $p < .05$, does not do anyone any favours. Surely what we want to know is whether there are genuine differences between our groups, and this is best answered when we have sufficient participants to actually test this.

With sufficient planning this type of study rarely goes wrong as it is a simple approach. If there is a good argument for using a between groups design, then it is a good place to start!

What are the practical issues associated with this method?

Most of these are described above. It can be hard to determine who the correct control groups are and then to recruit them. It can be hard to find appropriate measures that are still within the budget of the study. However, this is a straightforward method with very few additional practical issues to those encountered in all research.

Ethics

The usual ethical considerations apply: informed consent, managing risk, participant rights, and safety and best practice in data collection and storage. The main additional ethical consideration is whether you have different information sheets and consent forms for the different groups, or whether you have one. If you have more than one, you need to ensure you are clear that other groups are being recruited for the purpose of comparing the groups. Not doing this would amount to deception, as some groups may feel vulnerable in this kind of research. If you have one single information sheet and consent form, then you need to make sure there is a way to be clear with participants about which group you are considering them to be in. In considering your information sheets and consent forms you need to show sensitivities to all your participants.

Further reading

Any book that covers a variety of research methods in applied psychology will be helpful for this design as the key issues are common across a lot of approaches, participants and measures.

Lindsay, S. (2019). Five Approaches to Qualitative Comparison Groups in Health Research: A Scoping Review. *Qualitative Health Research, 29*(3), 455–468. https://doi.org/10.1177/1049732318807208
A great start when thinking about comparing groups in qualitative research.

9 Testing models in new groups

In Chapter 8, I discuss the issues with comparing constructs in different groups. One of the key problems with it is ensuring that the constructs you are comparing are meaningful. Sometimes you want to prove that the kinds of people you work with do deserve better services or kinds of services because they are more distressed or impaired or disabled by their conditions or difficulties. However, just showing that this is the case rarely leads to increased funding for the relevant services. It also isn't that interesting as a research question as it doesn't help us understand anything about why they are more distressed or impaired or disabled. A more interesting research question is how can we best understand distress or impairment or disability in different populations of people? One way of doing this is to ask them! This aligns well with qualitative approaches, so do see Chapters 11–14. However, if we are making arguments to commissioners about services, they may be more persuaded by numbers (they may be persuaded by both, so Chapter 15 on mixed methods is worth a read too). We also might have good ideas about why some people have greater distress or impairment or disability. We might have hypotheses about the impact of physical sensations on physical health (e.g., pain doesn't make you feel good). We might have hypotheses about their social worlds (e.g., looking different can lead to being ostracised and this doesn't feel good). We may have hypotheses about their environment (e.g., not being able to play/exercise outside if you have high energy leads to the energy being used in less constructive ways). Many of these hypotheses probably map onto theories that already exist out there in the world. So why would we trust other people's theories rather than develop our own? First, most theories are developed following a lot of work. Second, if there are theories in the literature there are quite likely to be measures that measure the constructs in those theories. This is crucial in testing theories in a valid and reliable way. Finally, if you explore theories in different groups, it becomes clear that theories are often developed in a way that does make them generalisable to other populations. Everyone is an individual, but our psychological processes overlap. You may not need to reinvent the wheel when there is a similar wheel to work with.

What is this approach?

This approach aims to test whether a full theory or model (see Box 3.1 for the difference between a theory and a model), or part of it, works when applied to another population. For example, you might take a model or theory that has been developed with adults and see whether it is relevant for children. You might take a model or theory that has been developed with people with asthma and see if it is relevant for people with diabetes. You might take a model or theory that has been developed to make sense of public institutions and see if it works for making sense of private institutions. Some theories already present themselves as not tied to a particular group of people, for example, coping theories or theories of resilience, but when you look at the research it may be that they have only been tested on certain groups of people and therefore it might be that we are simply unaware of its limitations when applied to other groups. An adaptation of this approach is to test and extend a model in a different population by adding variables that are relevant to your population.

Philosophy

If you test a model in a new population or extend a model in the population you are interested in, you are likely to do this quantitatively. Therefore, your philosophy is likely to be empiricist. However, as some parts of the model will fit better than others a realist philosophy is relevant to this method.

What kind of questions are best answered using this method?

If you are interested in this method, it is likely that you have a question about how something works in a particular group of people, but have not been able to find a theory, model or framework that has answered your question fully. You are probably interested in how different constructs interact with each other and how they apply to your population. The questions that are best answered using this approach involve the application of certain aspects of a model or theory to a novel population where it hasn't been tested yet, and where there is doubt as to whether the fit is good.

What are the key steps to using this method?

Identify your population. This method is most often used when you have a particular population in mind.

Identify suitable models or theories that might account for observations you have made about your population. There are several ways of doing this.
      You can *start with searches for the combination of your population and your construct*, for example, older adults with neurological impairment (population) and coping (construct), or infants (population) and fear (construct). If

you combine this with the words 'theory' 'model' or 'framework' then if there are models out there you are likely to find them. If you only find individual papers then these are also worth reading as the introduction to each paper has to make an argument for why the research was done, and you might find relevant theories or models in these arguments. If you find a theory or theories, then check out how well they fit with the question you are wanting an answer to.

If there isn't anything for your population, then **check out what populations your construct has been tested in**. For example, there might be theories of psychological adjustment after a certain kind of event or experience, and you are interested in a different event or experience. Your construct might only have been tested in psychology undergraduates, or only in adults aged 18–35 years. These models might be relevant enough to test in your population, or you might feel that there are good enough reasons for adding new constructs into the model. Adding new constructs should be driven by either a theoretical understanding of your population, or by empirical data. You can of course add in constructs that you have observed yourself and make a practical or clinical argument as to why you want to add them, but you have to make very good arguments that are convincing to others. This may be worth discussing with your research team.

If you still haven't found anything that fits well enough to even try testing with your population of interest then you may have to **create the model yourself**. You may find yourself leaning towards creating a model from scratch using something like grounded theory, or perhaps using reflexive thematic analysis, but the alternative is to synthesise the empirical literature to create a new model from what we already know (see Lawoko, 2007 for an example of this).

Map your model onto your new population to determine what the evidence is that it might be relevant to understanding the phenomenon of interest. There may be studies in the new population to map, or you may want to map the range of populations that the theory works for. This is important for your introduction, but also for truly understanding what might be the same and what might be different. It would be important at this stage to incorporate any evidence that suggests that the model isn't relevant to your population – either empirical evidence where a study has failed to find associations that are predicted, or any theoretical reasons why it isn't relevant, for example a theory that includes concern about food in an understanding of people with diabetes might theoretically not be as relevant for an understanding of people with asthma despite them both being chronic common illnesses.

Determine what aspects of the model you are going to test, and whether or not you are going to include additional variables not included in the original model. This step will be driven by your research question, where you might have a specific question about a specific part of a model, or you may just be interested in whether the model works for this new population. It will be impacted by the size of your potential participant pool. If you want to put lots of variables into your model you will need a larger sample size. If you truly want to test all aspects of a model, then consider using existing data (see Chapter 5) as this will give you the most power to test associations between different variables within the model.

Finally, this step will be determined by what you can measure. If you are testing an adult model in a child population your measures might not be appropriate and valid for your population. Similarly, if you are testing a very specific model with specific measures (e.g., diabetes related conflict, cancer-specific worry), then these are not likely to be relevant to other populations.

By this point in the planning process, you should have the **model mapped out** in your new population, highlighting the evidence for each association including the lack of evidence or contradictory evidence. You should have noted the most important aspects of the model to test, and what measures are available for each part of the model. The next step is to **calculate the sample size** needed to test the model or the parts of the model you want to test. You will need to understand what statistics you are likely to use, whether you are looking for associations (correlations), or whether you want to test which variables provide unique variance (regression), or whether you want to know how the variables work together in the model (path analysis or SEM, see Chapters 2 and 5 for discussion of sample size and statistics for testing models).

Source your participants and work with gatekeepers to **work out a recruitment strategy** (see Chapter 2). **Source your measures** that will measure the constructs you are interested in (see Chapter 8) and make sure you have written up all your research decisions so far to put in your introduction and method.

Finally, **carry out your study** and **write it up**.

How does this method usually go wrong and what can you do about it?

If this approach goes wrong, it is in the choice of model and/or measures, or in not managing to test the model well enough because of a small sample size. Therefore, the initial steps in planning the study, as described above, are crucial. If it is well planned, then this method can lead to a no-lose kind of study. If your statistics are significant and you can reject the null hypothesis, you have found a suitable model for your population. If you cannot reject your null hypothesis, then you have found that this model might not be suitable for your population, and you can hypothesise about why this might be the case. In terms of understanding your phenomenon in this population then both findings are useful knowledge.

What are the practical issues associated with this method?

These are addressed earlier in the chapter: choosing a relevant model and population, choosing good measures and recruiting sufficient participants to test the model appropriately. The solutions for these are all about good background research and good planning.

Ethics

The ethical issues are similar to those inherent in any research study; informed consent, confidentiality and anonymity, participants rights, managing risk, and data management.

Example: Applying adult models to adolescents

Wilson, C., & Hall, M. (2012). Thought Control Strategies in Adolescents: Links with OCD Symptoms and Meta-Cognitive Beliefs. *Behavioural and Cognitive Psychotherapy*, 40(4), 438–451. DOI:10.1017/S135246 581200001X

Martin was interested in obsessive-compulsive disorder, especially in adolescents. The cognitive model seemed appropriate for some of the adolescents he worked with, but something was missing, and he thought that the meta-cognitive model was worth exploring given his clinical experience using it with children and adolescents. Although Wells' (2017) meta-cognitive model of OCD hadn't been tested in adolescents, there was a meta-cognitions questionnaire that had been adapted for adolescents and we also found a single paper that had adapted the thought control questionnaire for use with adolescents (another important construct in the meta-cognitive model). OCD is a relatively rare disorder, and as it hadn't been tested in a younger population, we decided we would start by testing it in a community population. Martin knew he could invite a large secondary school to recruit participants for us and he anticipated a good response, which, with the support of the school management team, he got.

Although our original question was simply about thought control strategies and meta-cognitive beliefs and their association with OCD symptoms, we realised that we had a large enough data set to test an aspect of the model. We went back to the meta-cognitive model to see what the theoretical relationships were between thought control strategies, meta-cognitive beliefs and obsessive-compulsive symptoms and decided that we could test the mediation of thought control strategies and OCD symptoms by the meta-cognitive beliefs.

Further reading

Useful papers

Lucas, J. W. (2003) Theory-testing, generalization, and the problem of external validity. *Sociological Theory*, 21(3), 236–253.DOI: https://doi.org/10.1111/1467-9558.00187

Rocca, R., & Yarkoni, T. (2021) Putting psychology to the test: Rethinking model evaluation through benchmarking and prediction. *Advances in Methods and Practices in Psychological Science*, 4(3), 251524592110268. DOI: https://doi.org/10.1177/25152459211026864

Chapter references

Lawoko, S. (2007). Factors influencing satisfaction and well being among parents of congenital heart disease children: development of a conceptual model based on the literature review. *Scandinavian Journal of Caring Sciences*, 21(1), 106–117.

Wells, A., Myers, S., Simons, M., & Fisher, P. (eds) (2017). Metacognitive model and treatment of OCD. In *The Wiley Handbook of Obsessive Compulsive Disorders*, Volume 1, 644–662.

10 Observational research

NB: There are lots of studies that have observational in their title or abstract – this usually means they have recorded people's behaviour as it is, rather than manipulating it. This chapter is a bit different – it is about visually observing people's behaviour and systematically coding it.

In applied research we have often observed something in our practice that leads to the research question, however, when we come to create a method to answer our question we often try and find a different way of measuring the phenomenon, for example, using a questionnaire or survey, or interviewing people about their experience. However, these research methods cannot access all the data we might be interested in, and they move away from our original observation. Asking people about their experiences works best when these are experiences people are conscious of and can reflect on. We can access some unconscious processes through experimental design, for example by looking at reaction times or behaviour that betrays our implicit attitudes. However, often these designs lack external validity as they involve computer or digital responses, and the stimuli often must be simplified to allow them to be manipulated. For some research questions the best way of measuring our phenomenon of interest is to observe it directly.

What is this approach?

Observational research involves identifying our phenomena of interest, and systematically observing and coding what we observe. Typically, therefore, the phenomena we are interested in are those that are observable. These include verbal and physical behaviours, and interactions between people. Our observations should be robust, as should our coding of them, and we should take care to determine the context of our observations. In observational research we may be interested in how two variables are related to each other, for example how parental requests are related to child compliance. We might be interested in how two groups differ, for example in whether there are fewer pauses when conducting therapy online compared to conducting it in person. We might be interested in building an understanding of interactions within our observations, for example, whether parental requests accompanied by warmth are more likely to lead to child compliance, or whether there are only fewer pauses when conducting therapy online compared to in person when the therapeutic alliance is not very strong. Therefore, we can ask lots of different kinds of research questions in observational research.

Philosophy

Observational research may be part of qualitative enquiry, but it is more often done within a quantitative frame. As mentioned above, it can involve comparing groups, looking for relationships between variables, and model development. All these types of research questions come from empiricist and realist perspectives. The assumption underlying your observation is that you are observing something real about the person and by comparing groups or looking for associations between variables we are saying something real about the world. There can be all kinds of threats to validity of observational research (described below), so it is important that we consider these in our epistemology. People can change their behaviour when they are observed. The observational context, however real, also only captures a snapshot of behaviour. Therefore, a critical realist perspective may also be relevant. We will make choices as to what to code from our observations and we will make choices about what we call our coded behaviour. These all speak to our assumptions about the phenomenon and about our participants. We therefore play a part in taking a critical perspective on our data.

What kind of questions are best answered using this method?

The only questions that can really be answered by using this method are those where the phenomenon or phenomena in question can be observed, and to some extent quantified. What we do with this data depends on our research question and we can go on and analyse our data in whatever method works best for us. It may be that we are drawn to observational research when our participants are not necessarily the best people to ask about the phenomenon. This might be because of biases we all have in our natural cognition leading to biased recall or reporting, or because the phenomenon is not particularly available to introspection.

What are the key steps to using this method?

Decide on your research question. In order to determine what you are going to observe, when and how, you need to know what question you are going to ask. Observational research can have inductive as well as deductive elements to it as you may develop a coding system after you have your data. However, you need to know what question you are wanting to answer in order to set up the observations in the first place.

Decide what your phenomena of interest are. There may be work to do translating your research question into observable phenomena. For example, if you are interested in harsh parenting, how are you going to operationalise this? What behaviours make up harsh parenting? If you are interested in compassion, what aspects of compassion are you likely to be able to observe and how will you differentiate them from other forms of kindness or warmth?

Decide how to observe your phenomena of interest.

Where? Where are your participants going to be when you observe them? If you are interested in naturalistic behaviours you probably want to observe people in their natural environment. This approach maximises external validity, but there are threats to internal validity as each setting is likely to be different in potentially important ways that could impact the behaviour you are observing. If you want to maximise internal validity and observe behaviours within tighter constraints, for example within a manipulated experiment, then you need to find a way of constraining the external environment and it might be easiest to do this in a university lab, or room within a school or clinic.

When? Observational research often takes a significant amount of time. You need to set up equipment, make your participants comfortable, observe the behaviour you are hoping to see, and then debrief. It certainly takes a lot more commitment from you and your participants than giving out a short questionnaire. However, timing of your observations might be important. For example, some behaviours might be affected by circadian rhythms, and so you don't want to collect some data early in the morning and some late at night. Measuring these external variables is also helpful should you need to control for them during analysis.

For how long? This is determined by the research question and the behaviour you are interested in. If you are trying to observe something that happens regularly and frequently you may be able to observe your participants for a short time. If you are trying to observe something that is less frequent you may be able to manipulate the situation to encourage the behaviour. For example, when observing parent–child relationships we might get them to do something nice together like play with a toy or read a book, or something a bit more difficult together like talk about a difficult topic. The rarer the behaviour you want to see, the longer you need to observe your participants for. For some behaviours and for some populations just one observation session might be best, for example when your participants have a long way to travel to come to clinic or university, but for others it could be best to observe your participants a few times over different meetings, for example when it is helpful for them to feel comfortable or the behaviour is naturally very rare. How long you observe for influences your coding as you may count behaviours and use a frequency in your analysis, or you may want to control for the length of observation and use a rate (frequency divided by time).

With whom? In general, observations are best done with your participants only. However, it might be that you need other people to be there for safety, because it would be unethical not to (for example separating young children from their parents), or because it is part of your research question (for example introduction of the stranger in attachment observations). One situation you might need to consider is the situation where not everyone in the observation has given consent for you to observe them for research purposes. If you are observing a group, for example, some people in the group might either not be suitable participants or may not want to be part of the research. It is not ethical to observe people without their consent, however, some people in the group might be happy to be observed as long as their data isn't used for the research. If some people do not want to be observed and you cannot easily remove them from your observations you may need to choose a different setting where you can observe only people who have consented to take part. Some observations have the researcher as part of them as they can give instructions or be a stooge for an experiment, or can be part of a conversation, but other research questions would ideally not have the researcher as part of the observation. If this is the case, you might need to practise blending into the background. Children in particular seem very interested in strangers in their home or school who are trying not to talk to them!

Naturalistic vs non-naturalistic. Naturalistic settings maximise external validity, but compromise internal validity. They may also require larger sample sizes in order to account for variation in the frequency of behaviours observed. Non-naturalistic settings maximise internal validity at the expense of external validity but may require smaller sample sizes. It might be that there is a compromise you can do to achieve the balance you need.

Audio/video recording. There is a history in psychology of simply observing and then developing and testing theory. However, in a single research study this isn't likely to be helpful. You can observe your participants and do live coding of their behaviours. However, without any recordings of behaviours there are no governance checks, no way of testing inter-rater reliability, and no way of going back and making any changes should your coding system change. Recording has become less intrusive and more commonplace in everyday life, with people commonly recording aspects of their lives on their phones and other devices. The less intrusive the method of recording the more likely you are to get your participants behaving naturally. However, you also want to consider how to ensure your data is kept safely – carrying round recordings of your partici- pants on your phone is a bad idea! And you want your recording method to be reliable – having a device that could run out of charge before you have finished recording isn't a good idea! Whether you choose audio or video depends on your behaviour of interest. If you are interested in language or the behaviour you are coding depends on language, then an audio recording is sufficient. However, if you want to see what people are physically doing, then you will need a video recording. Most participants do not mind being recorded if this is stated up front. There are always some participants who are reluctant. Some of these will be less reluctant when you explain what it is for, who is going to see it, what you are looking for, and how safe you are going to keep it. However, there are always some people who will still be unhappy, and if your research question requires making recordings, then you will have to look elsewhere for participants.

Timing of getting additional information. While you are planning where you will observe your participants, doing what and for how long, you also need to think about what else you are asking of your participants and when you will ask them. Asking people to complete measures prior to being observed might exclude certain people or put them off, but asking them afterwards may risk having missing data if participants feel they have contributed enough by being observed. Plan round the weak spots in your research plan. If missing data will be very problematic then make sure you have questionnaires prior to making your observations. If you are comparing groups and you do know which groups people are in, then maybe focus on getting the observations done and ask for additional information after the observations.

Doing the observations. Once you have planned when, how, what and who, then there are some details to work through to ensure observations will go smoothly.

Equipment. What equipment do you need to successfully record your observations? Have you considered spare batteries, good quality audio, tripods or other ways of fixing your recording device?

Personnel. Are you able to do the recording yourself or do you need someone else with you? Having someone else there to do the recording can be more intrusive, but it can reduce the risk of errors in recording.

What to focus on. If you are recording behaviour, not just audio and language, then you need to consider what you will focus on if there are multiple people in your recording, such as parent–child dyads or a group of people. It may be that the recording can capture all the behaviour, but if it can't and participants may be able to walk out of shot, you need to have decided what to focus on should this happen.

Developing, choosing and/or adapting a coding system. For some phenomena there are existing high quality coding systems. In these coding systems there are codes and for each code there is a clear description of what constitutes an example of that code. It may be that there are also exceptions in the description. A good coding system also describes how the codes were developed and what the inter-reliability between different coders is. However, often there isn't a coding system that contains all the codes you are interested in. If this is the case, then you need to develop your own coding system or adapt an existing system so that it does include the relevant codes. Once you have developed your codes you need to think about the following aspects of your phenomena in order to work out how to code it from observations and transcripts.

Sampling frames, frequency, duration, intensity. Some phenomena that we observe are discrete individual behaviours, such as a sneeze or a handshake. These kinds of behaviours can be counted and the frequency of them might be most relevant to our question. Verbal behaviours can also be coded this way, perhaps how often someone uses a mental state term, or how often they say yes or no. However, for some behaviours it isn't helpful to record the frequency of the behaviour. For example, how long a child sits still for, or how long eye gaze is maintained between two people. These kinds of behaviours might be best recorded by their duration. Finally, some factors we want to record might be best recorded using their intensity such as the warmth of an interaction, or the strength of feeling in a conversation. Some behaviours might be composites, for example, turn-taking in conversation or sharing. Interacting with this aspect of coding (duration, frequency, intensity, composites) is the sampling frame. If you are going to observe naturalistic interactions then you might choose a time-limited frame, and observe each participant for the same amount of time. For some procedures participants may take different amounts of time and this impacts participants' opportunity to show different kinds of behaviours. If you are doing this, then you might want to calculate a rate of certain behaviours rather than a total frequency.

Recording sheets. Whether you are coding live, from a recording, or from a transcript, you want to develop a recording sheet. This could be a table with rows and columns. One of these is likely to represent time and the other the codes you are looking for. With this arrangement you watch or listen back to the recording and in each time-slot (which will depend on your codes) you identify whether the behaviour occurred in this time. An alternative is to have your transcript on one half of your paper, and to identify codes and write them in on the other side of the paper. There are some excellent coding programmes for certain kinds of data, such as CHAT and CLAN for coding language, and even qualitative analysis programmes such as NVIVO can be helpful for identifying all examples of a particular word or phrase.

Units of codes and combining codes. Some codes are composite codes. They do not neatly fit into a single event that happened or didn't. These are the kinds of codes that cannot be processed by a computer programme like NVIVO. They need you to make judgements about the nature of the behaviour prior to allocating a code to it. The other aspect of combining codes is to think about how you are going to combine codes for analysis. Imagine you end up with 20 different codes, then these act like different questions in a questionnaire. If you were going to develop a questionnaire from scratch, then you would probably use factor analysis to determine how your different questions are related to each other. However, you are very unlikely to gather sufficient data in an observational study to be able to do this with your codes. Instead, you are likely to combine your codes theoretically, based on your understanding of how the codes relate to each other. It is worth exploring your data to check that your theory is reasonable, usually by calculating Cronbach's alpha and possibly by inspecting the correlations between different individual codes.

Testing the coding system. Even when you have developed your coding system you need to check that it is reliable. Two main reliabilities that you can test are inter-rater reliability and test retest reliability. Inter-rater reliability is determined by how often two people code the same example of behaviour the same way. It can be tested using a Kappa statistic and usually is done with a portion of the coded behaviour, not all of it. Test–retest reliability in observational research is a test of whether coders rate the same behaviour in the same way if they code it at different times, for example, by reviewing a recording or transcript.

Answering the research question. In order to answer the research question you may need to combine codes to create the constructs you are interested in, and to test the reliability of these new combined codes. Once you have a reliable way of measuring your constructs you can go back to your research question and use appropriate descriptive and statistical techniques to answer it.

How does this method usually go wrong and what can you do about it?

If you are observing your participants, transcribing those observations, and then coding them, then it will take time. Lots of it. If you try and shortcut some of the important aspects, such as development of your coding system, or getting your participants used to the recording equipment, then you are likely to have problems further down the line. The only thing you can do about this is to take the time and make sure you have planned long enough for the different stages of your project. Observational work probably works better for longer projects where there is time to think about the alignment between your question, your observations and your coding system, and there is time to recruit your participants and spend enough time with them to ensure they are happy with what you are going to do.

Equipment is also a factor that can go wrong in observational work. Do you have spare batteries or some way of charging equipment if needed? How are you going to carry around all the equipment you need for the observations, especially if you are doing home visits? Or if you are observing something sensitive, consider how you are going to ensure that the recordings are kept safe, such as using lockable filing cabinets, password-protected recording equipment, etc.

The final thing that often goes wrong is coding. Once you start coding your observations you might find that the coding system doesn't have the codes you really need. There might be key aspects of your observations that aren't coded at all, or there may be codes that aren't working for your data or that you simply can't get inter-rater reliability on. The best thing to do here is to see the development of a coding system as an iterative process. The aim is not to create a coding system that gets the answer we want, but one that is able to answer the question we have. In order to counter issues such as p-hacking and harking, it is important that we are honest and transparent in describing our process of development of the coding system. Given that coding takes such a long time, then it is likely that we can undertake all iterations of our coding before we even start looking at testing our research question or hypothesis. This protects us against some aspects of bias, although we do need to try and be aware of our own biases in the development of the coding system.

What are the practical issues associated with this method?

Along with the time needed for good observational research, this kind of research can feel like some of the most equipment-heavy research you will ever do! You may be lugging bags and recording equipment round to people's houses. You may be taking encrypted laptops, recorders, and USB keys everywhere. Or you may be fighting with forms, pens, pencils, computer equipment and other electronic devices such as eye-tracking devices or heart monitors in the lab. It is never more than in observational research that you feel like you have to have a variety of skills that aren't your core research or psychology skills! If you have chosen this method, it is likely that you are happy (to some extent) doing this. The technophobes among us are very unlikely to choose this route for their research.

Ethics

Observing other people comes with a variety of ethical issues. Although there may be times when observing people without their consent is appropriate, it is unlikely that there are many of these. The kinds of grounds we might appeal to are legitimate interest or public interest. These might be appropriate for certain classes of data that are not sensitive, or do not involve any vulnerable person, but it is unlikely in most cases that collecting data without consent will be appropriate. Consent is therefore a crucial ethical issue. Do your participants know exactly what you are observing, and what you will be coding? Do they know who will have access to the recordings of them? When getting consent, is it fully informed?

Another crucial ethical issue is one of confidentiality and in observational research this is closely aligned with appropriate data collection, storage and processing procedures. In a video of someone their identity is obvious, and this could also be true of audio recordings. Once recordings, audio or video, are converted to transcripts we can fully anonymise our data, but prior to that we need to take care with those recordings.

The other important aspect of confidentiality is when it comes to breaking confidentiality. It is one thing for someone to talk about harm coming to themselves or someone else in a conversation where it can be addressed by the interviewee, it is another thing when harm is observed. It is important that prior to observations the research team has agreed exactly what the procedure is, should this happen. It is likely that it will not be considered ethical to act like a wildlife photographer and let the scene play out. It is more likely that recording must stop immediately, and the researcher should step in to stop any further harm from taking place. This must be done in a way that doesn't put the researcher in harm's way. In research where observing harm is more likely, it might be that two researchers need to be present at all times. Harm being directly observed during research may be a very rare occurrence, but that should not get in the way of having an appropriate plan should it happen.

As well as keeping data safe due to its lack of anonymity, it is up to the research team to determine what rights of access the participant will have. The Freedom of Information Act and related acts in other jurisdictions allow participants the right to access their personal data. Therefore, it may be that the researchers will need to be able to copy files, to allow participants access to these, and to determine what to do should other people be in the video or audio recording. This can be straightforward, and indeed giving participants a copy of a recording of them with a loved one may be a nice token of appreciation for participation. However, the recording could be of a group of people and therefore releasing this data would be subject to different data protection processes.

Ethics and social media research

With the rise of social media there has been a concordant rise in research that uses what people have posted on social media. Often this only involves using their own words, but with Instagram, Facebook stories and TikTok (three current ways of sharing videos) it is only a matter of time before researchers are using and debating the use of observed behaviour on social media. The debates about whether it is appropriate to use information that has been shared in a public forum will continue to rage, but as it is an ethical minefield guidance has been developed to help researchers think through the issues. As for every ethical consideration, the decisions are not straightforward or easy, but the guidance is helpful in thinking through the important issues and weighing up the pros and cons.

Example: Maximising opportunities in observational research

Wilson, C., Gardner, F., Burton, J., & Leung, S. (2007). Maternal Attributions and Observed Maternal Behaviour: Are They Linked? *Behavioural and Cognitive Psychotherapy*, 35(2), 165–178. doi:10.1017/S1352465806003195

Frances, my research supervisor, was interested in the protective role of positive and pro-active parenting behaviours in preventing the development of behavioural problems. She had planned a study of mothers and their three-year-olds which would involve collecting questionnaire and interview data, but that would also involve observing the mothers interacting with their three-year-old children. The study involved three home visits. The first involved getting to know the family, interviewing the mother about their child, and completing some questionnaires. In the second home visit, we observed the mother and child in a series of everyday tasks that we set up and asked the pair to complete, such as playing together and tidying up, and then preparing lunch. In the final home visit we asked mothers to spend an hour together doing what they would normally, except that we asked that the TV was turned off (there were no alternative screens back then!). I was able to fit some questionnaires and interview questions about their cognitions into the process in order to explore the relationship between their cognitions and behaviours. Within the study we observed parents and their children both in manipulated situations, in the everyday tasks we set up, and also in a more naturalistic setting: in their own home doing what they wanted. In this way we maximized the types of observations we made, and therefore could test a variety of research questions. Frances had already completed observational research and knew that there wasn't a coding system for coding the types of behaviours she was interested in. She therefore developed her own, with the researchers on the project developing inter-rater reliability prior to coding all the transcripts and answering the research questions.

Further reading

Books

Bakeman, R., & Quera, V. (2011) *Sequential Analysis and Observational Methods for the Behavioral Sciences*. Cambridge: Cambridge University Press.
Heyman, R. E., Lorber, M. F., Eddy, J. M., & West, T. V. (2014) Behavioral observation and coding. In *Handbook of Research Methods in Social and Personality Psychology*, 2nd ed. (pp. 345–372). Cambridge: Cambridge University Press.
Pellegrini, A. D. (2013) *Observing Children in Their Natural Worlds: A methodological primer*, 3rd ed. (pp. xviii, 322). New York: Routledge.
These books and chapters are a really good place to start to think about detail in observational research.

Papers

Aspland, H., & Gardner, F. (2003). Observational Measures of Parent-Child Interaction: An Introductory Review. *Child and Adolescent Mental Health, 8*(3), 136–143. https://doi.org/10.1111/1475-3588.00061
Gardner, F. (2000). Methodological issues in the direct observation of parent–child interaction: Do observational findings reflect the natural behavior of participants? *Clinical Child and Family Psychology Review, 3*(3), 185–198. DOI: https://doi.org/10.1023/A:1009503409699
These papers clearly have influenced my own work and are specific to parent-child interactions, but the issues discussed in them are relevant in lots of settings.

11 Thematic content analysis, template analysis and framework analysis

There are two main approaches to qualitative research in applied psychological settings. One approach takes a largely semantic approach with analysis that stays close to the words used by participants, and the other takes a more interpretative approach which focuses on understanding the meaning behind the words and the context of the participants' experiences. Both approaches are useful and answer different kinds of research questions. This chapter focuses on the semantic approach that focuses on content and on manifest themes, the three chapters following these focus on three different approaches to interpretative qualitative research that look to the meaning of participants' words and involve developing latent or underlying themes.

Thematic content analysis takes people's words and analyses them for their semantic and manifest content from the bottom up. Template or framework analysis starts with a template or framework about what you expect to find and then fit the data to this, looking for data that does fit and also data that doesn't.

What are these approaches?

Thematic content analysis (in contrast to reflexive thematic analysis) is a method of analysing qualitative data that stays close to the words being analysed with little interpretation. Sometimes it is used to summarise qualitative data into meaningful categories, and it can be used in conjunction with counting examples of each theme and sub-theme or coding qualitative data into quantitative data. Template and framework analysis also stay close to the words being analysed, but they foreground your assumptions and existing knowledge. They use what you know about the topic and what you expect to find in your data and use this knowledge to organise your data. You start with your template of what you think you might find, or your framework of what would be expected in the data, and you fit your open-ended exploratory data into it. The joy of template or framework analysis is that you can check to see if data fit existing theories while allowing space for new themes or parts of a theory or framework to be developed.

Philosophy

These kinds of approaches are often underpinned by a realist epistemology. If you are keen to stay close to your participants' words, with little interpretation, chances are you believe that the meaning is manifest (that is clear or obvious) in your participants' accounts of their experiences. This aligns well with a realist epistemology.

What is notable about the epistemology of these kind of approaches is that researchers who choose them often do not interrogate their positionality and epistemology as thoroughly as researchers who choose an interpretative approach. This is problematic, as the researcher will influence the analysis and results. Both template and framework analysis recognise this, acknowledge that we as researchers are subjective and hold biases and therefore make these biases and assumptions explicit. In thematic content analysis the biases and assumptions the researcher has can be dealt with through explicit statements of the philosophy of the study, through bracketing off of assumptions, and through adherence to more positivist values such as developing of a coding book and the calculation of inter-rater reliability.

What kind of questions are best answered using these methods?

These methods work well where there are qualitative data that need summarising into discrete themes. Thematic content analysis works well for exploring new research topics that do not have an established literature. Template and framework analyses work well when the topic is well explored, and you can easily predict what you might find. They also are useful when you want to know whether your data fit into an existing theory or framework. These methods work well for large qualitative studies or studies where the data is not rich and contextual.

The kinds of questions that are best answered by these methods are those that focus on experience, exploration, meaning and context. However, template and framework analysis might be particularly helpful for answering questions about whether a particular theory is relevant for a new population, or whether previously found constructs or factors can be found in a new context.

What are the key steps in using these methods?

Thematic content analysis

Thematic analysis is a very flexible approach in qualitative research. There are a number of adaptations to basic TA in psychotherapy research (Elliot and Timulak, 2015) in clinical psychology (Joffe, 2012), and in health psychology (Yardley, 2000). However, the steps involved in undertaking TA are similar.

Identify the research question. If you are considering Thematic Content Analysis (TcA) then you are probably expecting your data to be in the form of words, and you are probably interested in your participants' experiences. Your research questions may therefore focus on describing or summarising participants' experiences, exploring a new phenomenon to find the important aspects of it, or synthesising data into meaningful concepts.

Collect your data. Most qualitative data is collected using interviews or focus groups. However, there are lots of different options for collecting qualitative data (see Braun, Clarke and Grey, 2017). If you want to focus on synthesising your data and make conclusions about importance based on how many participants mention key concepts, then it is important that each participant gets the same opportunity to comment. This might drive how you collect your data; you may want a more structured interview where there are a set of questions that each participant is asked rather than an unstructured interview. Most qualitative interviews are described as semi-structured. This means that there are key questions that the researcher will ask, but researchers will have the opportunity to ask the participant additional questions if there is something they really want to talk about that is relevant to the research question. In qualitative research that stays close to the words used then the researcher will follow more closely the interview schedule and allow participants to talk about their own agenda less frequently. There may therefore be more questions in the interview schedule and the approach the interviewer takes may be more direct.

Focus groups can be very helpful in certain circumstances. Some participants may feel more able to participate in a group as there is less pressure on them to 'perform'. In addition, the experiences of other focus group members can prompt participants to remember important aspects of their own experience. It may prompt agreement or disagreement, thus enhancing the richness of the data. However, focus groups designed to collect data for synthesis do need to ensure each participant has the same opportunities to answer each question. This can remove some of the benefits of focus groups. Facilitating focus groups also takes a different set of skills and novice researchers with few group facilitation skills may struggle to balance the demands of the research with managing the group dynamic. Applied psychology practitioners, however, may have excellent group facilitation skills and may find focus groups a suitable method for collecting data.

Braun and Clarke suggest a wide range of additional methods of collecting data, including excellent guidance on using qualitative surveys. These can be helpful for both thematic content analysis and reflexive thematic analysis (see Chapter 12) and are particularly relevant in mixed methods studies in applied psychology.

Transcribe your data. If you are staying close to the words of your participants and their semantic meaning (in contrast to their implicit or implied meaning) then the most important thing in transcription is the words. Other qualitative analysis approaches may require you to transcribe pauses, non-verbal utterances, and even notate transcriptions with mood or comments on non-verbal processes. However, for this kind of analysis, the important thing is the words. Transcribing your own interviews may take a long time, but it is a crucial early part of analysis. While transcribing your interviews or focus group recordings you notice responses that you didn't notice while collecting the data. You can spot recurring ideas and concepts, and you can notice unusual responses that might counter other experiences. Transcription is a long and painstaking process, and therefore seeing it as the first step in analysis can help you get through it! (See Chapter 13 for more discussion of issues in transcription.)

Start the analysis. One of the key aspects of quality in qualitative research is the robustness of the analysis. This involves systematically going through all your data to identify codes and themes. Some approaches call this line-by-line coding, but a line depends on too many things – your font size, your page orientation, your margins, or if you are taking a line to mean a sentence that is spoken, then it depends on the speech patterns of your participant. Some participants do not speak in sentences! It may be more obvious to code each meaningful chunk of data. Each chunk of meaningful data should be allocated a code. The code should make sense independently of the data in that the code you have used should mean something to you even if it is separated from the data. However, as you go through your coding if you are re-using codes you can start to use a shorthand for yourself. You should go through all your data to look for suitable codes. Even in the final transcript you code you might find new codes that are important for your understanding. A code should be a summary of the data chunk; see Table 11.1 for examples of codes.

Continue the analysis – starting to identify themes. The next step is to review all your codes. You might do this by looking at them separately to your data, or it might be that you have good ideas as to the common codes and want to write them down first and then look for others that aren't as frequent or salient. You want to collect the similar ones together and start to give names to these potential themes.

Refine and finalise themes. At this stage you probably have too many themes. There are several ways to reduce them. You can map your themes to see how they fit together and see if any of them can be put together into a single theme. You can use memos to describe your themes (see Chapter 13 on Grounded Theory) and in the descriptions you may find similarities that allow you to combine themes. You may go back to the theory or framework and work out how the themes fit best. This is the stage where supervision or discussions with colleagues or collaborators can be crucial. You have been working with your data for a while now, and it might be hard to make difficult decisions about combining or rejecting themes.

Find quotes and write up your results. In your results section the themes will be described, quotes will be provided to evidence the theme, and the organisation of the order and priorities of the themes and sub-themes will be determined. Mapping themes helps with this final process. You may want to integrate your results and discussion and draw on the existing literature and theory in the description of your themes, or you may want to keep them separate.

Template analysis

Template analysis has been developed largely by Nigel King and his website is a great resource for all things template analysis (see below for link). These stages are adapted from his account of how to do template analysis.

Define the themes you expect to find (a priori themes) based on your existing knowledge, existing theory and empirical evidence. It is worth writing a reflexive account of this – where did the ideas for themes come from? What kind of evidence do you have for them? Did you think of calling them something different and why? How do you think they relate to each other?

Collect and transcribe your data. This is the same process as described for the thematic analysis.

Become familiar with your data. This might involve transcribing your interviews or reading carefully through your survey data.

Go through your data and code each codable unit. This might be a sentence, or a couple of sentences. You can assign each code to one of your a priori themes and make a note of those codes that don't fit into any current theme. I tend to have highlighters on hand for this if working on paper and I use the highlight function if working in Word.

Identify which codes do not fit into your a priori themes and determine whether you need to add a new theme or whether you can modify an existing one. This is another stage where reflexive accounts are helpful. What were your thoughts in developing a new code? Did you think it might fit somewhere else and why did you decide that it didn't?

On either the whole dataset or a part of it **develop an initial template**. This has your a priori themes and new themes in it but it also describes how they relate to each other. The themes should be arranged hierarchically. You will have some higher order themes and sub-themes.

Fully develop your template using all your data. Modify your theme descriptions, add detail, determine the relationships between higher order and lower order themes more fully.

With this final template, **write up your findings.**

Framework analysis

Framework analysis has many similar steps although it uses a different language and a more structured process. Familiarisation, the steps of developing the framework and mapping the data onto the framework are like the steps described above. However, in framework analysis data is sifted, charted and sorted. Sifting your data involves choosing the data to create the framework. Charting and sorting involves organising all your data into a matrix that is developed in the familiarisation and sifting phases and involves careful analysis of each participant's data. This matrix is your framework with your themes as column headings and your participants in each row. The themes/categories or column headings can be influenced by your existing expectations and under-standing of your phenomena.

How many themes should I have?

The number of themes can be determined by a number of different factors:

The approach you are taking to your analysis. If you are trying to sum-marise verbal data into appropriate categories your interviews and resulting data will determine how many themes. This is because you will want to sum-marise all data that are relevant to answering your research question. This is the approach that is most likely to result in a large number of categories with possibly several levels of sub-themes. If you are wanting to describe important themes, then there are likely to be fewer themes.

Your research question. Your research question might be quite open-ended, for example 'what are the experiences of people with type 2 diabetes of exercise?', or it might be more closed-ended, for example, 'what are the experienced mechanisms of change in compassion focused psychotherapy for people with low self-esteem?'.

The time available to analyse your data. More experienced researchers, and researchers with time to set the results aside and come back to them, will see ways in which a more coherent streamlined set of themes can be developed. However, this isn't always possible if you are undertaking applied research as part of a qualification.

NB: if you have lots of themes it might be you need to spend more time with your data. It can be a symptom of the analysis not being complete!

What is the difference between a code and a theme?

A code is a word or short phrase to capture the essence of a small part of your data. A theme is a category within your data that captures repeated parts of your data. In thematic content analysis you can have as many levels of themes as makes sense for your data, so some themes might provide an overall description of a large part of your data, whereas sub-subthemes might provide a description of a sub-set of that theme. E.g., in Figure 11.1 the overarching

Figure 11.1 A hierarchy of themes: an example

Overarching theme: Emotional responses to loss					
Sub-theme: Positive responses			Sub-theme: Negative responses		
Sub-sub-theme: Acceptance	Sub-sub-theme: Post-traumatic growth	Sub-sub-theme: Sadness	Sub-sub-theme: Guilt	Sub-sub-theme: Shame	Sub-sub-theme: Anger

Table 11.1 Examples of codes from a short participant extract

Narrative from participant	Examples of codes
Well I guess I was angry for a long long time. I don't think I knew why I was angry, but it spilled out everywhere. Oh my God! I was angry at my kids, I was angry at my partner, I was angry at the person who sells me coffee even. But then it just, well, kinda changed. I think maybe I started letting it in just a bit, erm, feeling the feelings, you know. And then the sadness kicked in. I think I also started to accept it a bit if you know what I mean. I think, well, erm, I think that's where the sadness came from. I had so many memories and they kept popping up when I didn't expect them. I'd be there in the queue for my shopping and I'd just be in tears thinking – they'll all think I'm a mad woman! I think I felt guilty at all the things I should have done at the end. I just kinda couldn't deal with it all and I pushed it away, it was just too much you know? Well, erm, I...{tails off, pause}	Anger, persistent anger Generalised anger Letting the feeling in Feeling the feeling Sadness, accepting the loss Sadness Intrusive memories Sadness and tears, thinking others think she's mad, guilt Pushing it away Too much
I'm in a different place now. I'm trying to be kinder to myself about it. My therapist helped with that, she said – what would you say to a friend – and I realised I was being much nastier to me than I would be to anyone else. That's amazing too cos I can see me doing that in other, erm, in other bits of my life. I still feel really guilty about, those, erm, those last days... I guess I'm a bit ashamed I ran away from it all and couldn't deal with it. I thought I was a stronger person than that. But therapy is really helping. I'm a different person now. Stronger.	Self-kindness Therapy being helpful Self-kindness in life more generally, guilt Shame Therapy is helpful Stronger now

theme is emotional responses, with these split into positive and negative, and these in turn split into acceptance and post-traumatic growth, and into sadness, guilt, shame, and anger.

Table 11.1 displays a short extract from just one participant. Their words don't match exactly the themes that were developed, but you can see key words and key concepts starting to emerge in the codes chosen. The codes are short and stay close to a semantic reading of the participant's words. Some of the codes become themes directly, some are combined with others to develop slightly different themes, for example, 'stronger now' becomes 'post-traumatic growth'. In thematic content analysis you should have a short description of each theme so that someone else looking at the transcripts could identify that theme from the participants' words.

How many participants or how much data?

Most researchers associate qualitative research with small numbers of participants. However, you need to consider your research philosophy to see whether this is true for the qualitative approach you are taking. If you are exploring a new area and want to make conclusions about the area of interest or topic, then you need sufficient data and sufficient participants to do so. If you want to capture key aspects of a phenomenon and categorise them into useful themes and categories, again you need sufficient data and sufficient participants to ensure you have captured relevant aspects of the phenomenon. In general, you will need more participants in a thematic content analysis to make it valid than you will in constructionist and interpretative approaches because you are making different claims about the truth and reality of your findings. You might need to balance numbers of participants with representativeness of your participants. For example, if you are asking open-ended questions about the acceptability of an intervention, you cannot simply ask the people who responded well to it and then conclude that there were lots of great things about your intervention. In interpretative approaches you are looking for underlying meaning, and for descriptions of context for your findings, but in semantic approaches you are looking for frequency and importance of categories and themes, so you need to give your participants enough time and space to give you this information, and you need enough participants to be able to make conclusions about these two domains.

To saturate or not to saturate

Saturation is a concept borrowed from Glaser's version of Grounded Theory (see Chapter 13 for discussion of this in this context) and refers to the situation where no more themes can be developed from the data. In Grounded Theory themes need to be considered along lots of different dimensions/qualities in order to create a theory. In Grounded Theory saturation can require further collection of data in order to determine these qualities, however, that is rarely the case in thematic content analysis where saturation can be achieved by ensuring that all the relevant data are captured by the themes described.

In reality when people say they have analysed their data until saturation, they mean they have done a thorough analysis. This is because there are some difficulties with the concept of saturation (see further reading below), including the relevance of saturation across different types of qualitative analysis, how to square saturation with answering a research question which might have a tighter focus than the answers participants gave, and how to know when you have reached saturation. People write sentences like 'Analysis proceeded until no new categories or themes emerged, and saturation was reached'. I'm often a little sceptical of this as whenever I go back to data I can create new themes from it by taking a different perspective.

However, the principle of carefully going through all your data, coding each line, chunk or concept within it, and then systematically going through the codes to create categories/themes is a good one! By the time you have completed your analysis I would expect you to really know your dataset inside out, and have strong, evidenced views about what you want to say about your participants' experiences or views.

How do these methods usually go wrong and what can you do about it?

The main thing that goes wrong with this method is that the research question, the interview questions, the number of participants and the analysis do not all **align**. As you can see, there is a lot to align! But thematic content analysis has much more in common philosophically with quantitative research than it does qualitative research, and yet as it is written about as a qualitative approach, people tend to treat some of the other assumptions the same as interpretative qualitative approaches. If you want to make claims about how the world really is, and what your participants' experiences are, then you need sufficient participants, to give each participant equal opportunity to comment on the topic, and you need to develop frequent and important themes that could be identified by other researchers. That might involve developing a code book, or it might involve inter-rater reliability. You need data that is sufficiently detailed to answer your research question. Good research interviewing comes with practice and, if possible, with supervision. You can often be your own best supervisor, listening back to interviews and determining yourself what you can change next time. A colleague or academic supervisor with experience in interviewing for qualitative analysis can also be helpful.

If you have all the important elements of your research aligned, then the main issues occur in the **coding**. Psychologists can easily be pulled into taking a more interpretative approach, which may not be suitable for the data or for answering the research question. Another common problem in coding is having too many themes. Often it is hard to give up certain codes and if they don't easily fit into existing themes the obvious solution can be to develop new themes. If your thematic map is getting more and more complex with more levels and complex relationships between themes and sub-themes, it is worth taking the next step in analysis and trying to simplify. This can be less of a problem using template or framework analysis, but in all approaches involves making active decisions about what levels of the thematic map need to be described. You might have a complicated tree of themes in your head and in your rough work, but you might not have space or want to describe all the branches. Remember, you need to answer your research question. Often this problem occurs early in analysis and what you need to do is to take a break, leave it for a week or two, and then come back to it with fresh eyes. It is amazing what your brain will do while you are not thinking about it!

In template or framework analysis some of the things you might think are 'going wrong' in your coding are in fact not going wrong at all. If you find that your original themes are completely off, and you must develop new themes, that is fine. It is a useful finding. If you find that all your codes fit into existing themes and there is no inductive work to be done, then you were right – the existing literature is a good representation of the field.

Finally, in terms of your **write up**, you need to decide what role quotes are going to have in your write up (see Box 11.1) and how you will include them in your work. Often, they are embedded within the text, but for these kinds of approaches tables of themes with illustrative quotes may be appropriate.

Box 11.1: Story book or frontispiece

I often characterise the write up of a qualitative analysis as the author's writing being the words and the participant quotes being the pictures or illustrations. Think about the kind of picture books designed for young children that have no words at all. They encourage children to make up the story themselves, while structuring the illustrations so that there is a story, there is a flow and so most children will come up with similar stories about the pictures. For this to happen the pictures themselves have to be excellent and the arrangement of them has to be skilful, and well-planned and executed. Then think about the other end of the spectrum where beautiful old books have no separate illustrations, but then you come across a page or two of illustrations in the middle of the book that capture some key scenes, or they simply have the first letter of the first word of each chapter illustrated. Most of the story unfolds with the author's words, but occasionally there is an illumination of these using a picture that brings it to life.

Writing up qualitative research can be done in either of these ways. We can foreground participants' voices by reporting our themes mostly as quotations from participants, or we can foreground our own thinking and analysis by writing about the themes and using quotations sparingly for illustration.

Both of these approaches are good ways of writing up qualitative research, but they achieve different aims and are based in different philosophies. The metaphor is useful as it may help you think about what kind of paper you want to write about your participants' experiences. You could try writing your results section in both extremes and to then read each to see what you like about it and what you don't. This exercise can really help you see what you want to write and what your own personal style is in qualitative research.

What are the practical issues involved in these methods?

These are very flexible research methods! They are flexible with respect to your participants; they are flexible with respect to data collection. Therefore, the practical issues involve data and time management. You will have more participants than other researchers taking more interpretative approaches (in general), but your data will be words, then codes, then themes. You need to keep on top of all of these! In template and framework analysis it can feel strange to write down what you expect of your data; somehow it feels a little like cheating. However, it is an important part of the process that, in the end, will result in a better analysis and better set of results.

The other aspect of organisation is the development of a code book, inter-rater reliability, and tracking changes to your template or framework as you develop it. As you create your codes and develop them into themes and sub-themes you need to keep track of what they mean and what the boundaries between different themes are. In developing an intermediate template, you might ask how much analysis is enough and 'Should I code the whole dataset before I edit the template?' and there are no hard and fast rules about this. If you edit your template early then you risk having many versions of it, but if you wait till you have re-coded all your data you may miss some of the nuance by waiting till you have all your main findings in your head. If you are wanting to double-check your analysis and get someone else to do the inter-rater reliability you need to find that person and train them! This may be relatively easy if you are working within a research team, but if you are not, for example, when you are a student, it might be harder to do. It might be that you have to find someone who needs their inter-rater reliability done and do each other's!

Ethics

As well as the usual ethical considerations of informed consent, managing risk, anonymity and confidentiality, keeping data well and protecting participants' rights there are a few additional things to think about in the ethics for qualitative research.

Pseudonyms. It is helpful in your write up to use identifiers for any quotations you use. This allows the reader to see which participant accounts are being used to evidence your themes and to see if you are drawing on a wide range of participants, or a few. There are always one or two participants that you could use in every theme as they eloquently describe their experience. However, if you only use those two participants to provide evidence for all your themes then it may be you have privileged those accounts and not paid enough attention to the participants who may not be as eloquent. However, how you name these identifiers is an interesting ethical issue. Using participants' actual names breaks confidentiality. However, this might be ethical if participants consent to it and it does value the participant's time and effort. Some participants prefer to be named once they have taken the trouble to take part. Often pseudonyms are used. These can be chosen carefully by researchers to reflect cultural, gender, and class differences in the participants, but if not chosen carefully may reflect researchers' biases rather than being neutral. Some researchers have asked participants to choose their own pseudonyms, but you have to be prepared to use the names of famous actors, musicians and social media stars!

Another alternative is to choose numbers for participants. This isn't subject to researcher biases, but it can dehumanise the data. For non-interpretative approaches this may not be a problem, but it could be more of a problem for interpretative or reflexive approaches (see Chapter 12 for more).

Analysis and informed consent. Another ethical issue in this kind of qualitative research is considering what participants are expecting to happen to their data. Some participants will express a preference for taking part in an interview as they have a chance to explain themselves, but it may be more mysterious what might happen to their data in the analysis process. This is something that can be addressed in the information about the study and the consent form.

Boundaries round qualitative interviews. A final ethical issue that it is important to consider is whether participants end up sharing information they regret. In the middle of an interview this might be quite easy, especially with a skilled interviewer. Some approaches in qualitative research invite participants to review their own transcript and to redact anything they are not happy being analysed. However, sometimes there isn't time, and sometimes it isn't appropriate. In which case tuning into participants' experiences during the interview and a careful debrief process might address this ethical issue.

Example: What to do with very large samples in qualitative research

Bhreathnatch, L., Wilson, C., Lowry, D., Mulhearn, S., Hevey, D., O'Sullivan, S., O'Doherty, V., D'Alton, P., Pender, N. (2021). "It was like war": An Investigation for the Negative and Positive Experiences of Healthcare Workers During the COVID-19 Pandemic. Paper presented at the Psychological Society of Ireland Conference, 2021

When COVID-19 hit Ireland everything turned upside down. We were sent home from schools and colleges one Thursday, and then a week later the country went into full lockdown. My main job was in training people for the health service, and as they were psychologists most had been sent to work from home. However, some colleagues were still in hospitals and clinics being deployed to other departments and other roles. I wanted to understand their experience and luckily, I was not alone. I quickly found that other people, especially those directly affected, were also worried and keen to understand the impact of the pandemic on health care workers. Coming together from different hospitals we negotiated what kind of research project we wanted to do. It felt important to measure the key outcomes that were already coming out of studies like ours, such as stress, trauma, anxiety and depression, but there was also a keen interest in what we weren't capturing in these data. We added some questions in our survey about coping and about how things were before the pandemic, but there was good support across the team to ask a few very simple open-ended questions. I did not want to pre-judge all the outcomes to be negative, so when we added a question about what had the negative effects of the pandemic been, I also wanted to add whether there had been any positive effects. We also decided to ask about coping because it felt to us that all coping measures are problematic in some way, and we also finished our survey with an open-ended question inviting participants to tell us anything else they wanted to.

What made the analysis complex was the sheer number of participants. We wanted to get about 500 people, and in the end we had over 2300 participants. Linda expressed interest in looking at the data for her master's research and she didn't seem daunted by the number of participants. I anonymised the data, making decisions about what did and what didn't constitute identifiable data. We decided to use a thematic content analysis in order to best represent the content of the data. We had a great deal of data, but not all of it was rich. We also wanted to stay close to the experience and the words of the participants rather than try and interpret them in the context of a very difficult global situation.

Due to time limitations, we decided not to create a code book, nor explicitly get inter-rater reliability. We discussed the codes and themes at each stage to ensure that they mapped well onto the data. Anonymising the data helped with this process as it meant that both Linda and I had spent time reading and processing the data. There were certainly challenges in coding data from such a large number of participants, but the meaningfulness of the themes made it worthwhile.

Further reading

Thematic content analysis

Boyatzis, R. E. (1998). *Transforming Qualitative Information: Thematic Analysis and Code Development.* Thousand Oaks, CA: SAGE.

Elliott, R., & Timulak, L. (2015). *Descriptive and interpretive approaches to qualitative research* (Vol. 1). Oxford: Oxford University Press. DOI: https://doi.org/10.1093/med:psych/9780198527565.003.0011

Joffe, H. (2012). Thematic Analysis. In D. Harper & A. Thompson (Eds.), *Qualitative Research Methods in Mental Health and Psychotherapy: A Guide for Students and Practitioners.* (pp. 209–223). Chichester: Wiley-Blackwell.

Yardley, L. (2000). Dilemmas in qualitative health research. *Psychology & Health,* 15(2), 215–228. DOI: https://doi.org/10.1080/08870440008400302

Template and framework analysis

Brooks, J., McCluskey, S., Turley, E., & King, N. (2015). The Utility of Template Analysis in Qualitative Psychology Research. *Qualitative Research in Psychology,* 12(2), 202–222. DOI: https://doi.org/10.1080/14780887.2014.955224

King, N. (1998). Template analysis. In *Qualitative methods and analysis in organizational research: A practical guide* (pp. 118–134). London: Sage Publications Ltd.

Srivastava, A., & Thomson, S. B. (2009). Framework analysis: A qualitative methodology for applied policy research. *4 Journal of Administration and Governance 72,* 8.

Also check: https://research.hud.ac.uk/research-subjects/human-health/template-analysis/

A classic text on focus group research

Morgan, D. L. (1996). Focus groups. *Annual Review of Sociology*, 22(1), 129–152.

Chapter reference

Braun, V., Clarke, V., & Gray, D. (Eds.). (2017). *Collecting qualitative data: A practical guide to textual, media and virtual techniques.* Cambridge: Cambridge University Press.

12 Reflexive thematic analysis

Thematic analysis is perhaps the most widely used qualitative approach in psychology. However, it is perhaps also the most misunderstood. One of the errors, which I have just made myself, is to describe thematic analysis as a single approach. Thematic analysis can be used to summarise data within a positivist philosophy (see Chapter 11), but Braun and Clarke's work on thematic analysis since their seminal paper on it in 2006 has revolutionised how it can be used to analyse qualitative data. Only in the most recent book have Braun and Clarke renamed their approach to distinguish it from other approaches. Thus, this chapter aims to represent their work, and their approach to thematic analysis which is Reflexive Thematic Analysis.

What is this approach?

Reflexive Thematic Analysis (RxTA)[1] is a flexible approach to collecting and analysing qualitative data that aims to develop a meaningful understanding of participants' experiences and represent them in rich descriptive themes. It is flexible in its philosophy, in its collection and use of data, and in its analysis. It goes beyond a content-based thematic analysis as described in Chapter 11 to develop themes that describe meaningful aspects of the phenomenon and that answer the research question in a way that foregrounds meaning and context. The word 'reflexive' indicates that this type of TA involves critical thinking about your role as researcher and the process of doing qualitative research as well as being reflexive within your analytic process.

Philosophy

Reflexive Thematic Analysis can be used with a variety of philosophies from realist to relativist ontologies and from contextualist to constructionist epistemologies. It lends itself to these different perspectives as it does not restrict itself to one way of looking at the world. Indeed, Braun and Clarke (2022) suggest that a successful orientation to RxTA involves 'The ability to embrace the idea that knowledge comes from a position, and a disinterest in the idea of a singular universal truth

---

[1] RTA is too well known an acronym to be used for Reflexive Thematic Analysis, and therefore I am using RxTA. This isn't common nomenclature, but hopefully it makes sense in the context of this chapter.

to be discovered' (p7). There is a rejection of positivist ideas and a singular truth to be discovered, but beyond that, there can be flexibility and you have to decide what your own understanding of truth and knowledge are. If you are coming from a largely quantitative tradition and training then the idea that there is a reality out there, but an acknowledgement that there is not a single way of knowing it, is a relatively short step from how reality and truth are considered in your training. However, if you are coming from a largely qualitative tradition, the idea that reality and truth are relative and constructed in our relationships within our use of language might feel very comfortable to you. One of the benefits, and joys, of RxTA is that it can allow for different philosophical positions. One of the challenges with this, however, is that you have to determine what your own position is.

What kinds of questions are best answered using this method?

RxTA is a very flexible method, and therefore any qualitative question such as 'what are people's experiences of ...?', 'what is the meaning of <topic> for people?', 'how do people make sense of...?', 'what are people's perspectives on ...?', are all good questions for RxTA. Braun and Clarke highlight that your research question can start broad, but should be encompassing of the wider political context, the existing literature and the scope of the dataset. As you collect and analyse your data, you might find that aspects of your question narrow or sharpen, or you take part of your dataset as it relates to your overall question best.

Box 12.1: Thematic Content Analysis (TcA), Reflexive Thematic Analysis (RxTA) or Interpretative Phenomenological Analysis (IPA)?

Question	Decision
Do you think there is a *right* answer or set of answers in your data?	This is a positivist view and therefore TcA is best.
Is your interest in experience about really focusing in on the individual or are you interested in patterns across the dataset?	If you are interested in individuals primarily then IPA might suit better. If it is more about the shared experiences and patterns across different people's experiences, then RxTA is probably better.
How many participants may you be able to recruit?	If you know that you have a restricted dataset in terms of numbers, then avoid TcA as you may not be able to make the kinds of conclusions you want to.

Question	Decision
How tight is your focus on the topic?	If you are interested in a particular phenomenon and really want to get to understand it fully, then choose IPA. If you are interested in unpacking the wider picture and including different experiences and different perspectives to get a better understanding of the wider context, then choose RxTA.
How willing are you to challenge your own assumptions and spend time thinking about your own processes in relation to the data?	If you have not got the time, emotional energy or external support to be very reflective, then TcA will be better for you.
Do you find yourself wanting to know numbers of participants who endorsed each theme?	You need TcA.
How comfortable are you sitting with uncertainty?	If you really struggle with this, then TcA might be best as the process will hold the uncertainty for you. IPA is probably best of the interpretative approaches because the focus on the individual can block out some of the bigger aspects of uncertainty. For RxTA you need to be able to sit with uncertainty quite comfortably.

TcA: Thematic Content Analysis; RxTA: Reflexive Thematic Analysis; IPA: Interpretative Phenomenological Analysis. *NB: This box doesn't include Grounded Theory as an approach because the questions asked are usually substantially different.*

What are the key steps in using this method?

Determine your research question. Although RxTA can answer almost any question for which qualitative research is appropriate (see Box 12.1 for some examples of how to decide this), there are some questions that are particularly suited to RxTA. These include research questions that focus on meaning and context, and ones where there might be divergent views and experiences.

Determine who your participants will be. In RxTA your participants can be whoever will help you answer your research question. There is no requirement for homogenous participants (like IPA) or to find exceptions (like Grounded Theory). You can do quality RxTA with relatively small numbers of participants (for example, 6–8) and you can do quality RxTA with very large numbers of participants (for example, 100s). This does make RxTA a good method to choose if you want to take an inclusive stance in your research. RxTA also allows different methods of collecting data such as combining interviews with focus group and open-ended online surveys. This also can promote inclusivity of different kinds of participants with different abilities and different preferences. In qualitative research there are fewer ways of collecting data from non-verbal participants than there are of collecting data from participants who express themselves verbally. RxTA can deal with all of this.

Collect your data. There are lots of qualitative approaches that allow or encourage you to think broadly about your data collection strategy, but it is rare that the authors of the approach explicitly write about different ways of collecting data. In their book with Debra Grey, Ginny Braun and Victoria Clarke discuss story completion, diary approaches, blogs and online discussion forums, and use of email or asynchronous messaging. Even if you know you want to do interviews or focus groups it is worth considering the method by which you collect the data more widely to encourage yourself to be creative even within your interviews.

Transcribe your data. Transcription is hard. It is both boring and high stakes, which is the worst combination! However, it is invaluable as a first step in analysis. It is possible to get your interviews transcribed for you and if you aren't asking about very sensitive issues and you are either pushed for time or have lots of money to throw at the study, this might be a good option for you. Otherwise, you are going to do it yourself. There are exceptions to this of course. If you are a researcher with disabilities that precludes doing your own transcription, then it makes most sense to get someone else to transcribe your interviews. These are not limited to physical disabilities but include disabilities that would make auditory processing or multi-tasking or typing difficult.

Getting someone else to transcribe your interviews for you. If someone else will be listening to your interviews then this needs to be included in data protection assessments, in the information sheets for participants and possibly in the consent forms. You will want to listen through to your interviews before you send them off for transcription to ensure that there isn't anything that breaches any data protection issues and might therefore require editing. It is worth doing your homework about who to send them to and how good they are at transcribing to the level you need because transcription services vary widely. You want a transcriber who shows great accuracy, provides good detail, and only denotes a few sections 'could not hear'. When you get your transcripts back you will want to check them against the audio recording to check for accuracy and detail. This might seem long-winded, but it is still quicker than transcribing them yourself!

Transcribing interviews yourself. Thinking about transcription starts with thinking about *how you are going to record your interviews*. By using good equipment you can save yourself lots of time during transcription. In recent times, while we have connected over our computers, there has been a rise in videoed research interviews, some of which come with transcription. However, the quality of this varies and it is worth doing some trials to check what the best way of recording your interviews is.

Next you probably need to decide whether you *are going to use any technology to help you with your transcription.* A transcription pedal can be helpful, with the ability to rewind, slow down as well as start and stop with your foot while your hands are typing. You might benefit from specific software that can facilitate transcription or it might just be that you choose what equipment you are going to use to play the interviews and what equipment you are going to use to type them up. If you have recordings on the computer for example, then it might be harder to control the audio as well as typing as you will be going between different computer programmes. For some research questions and datasets there are specific programmes you can type straight into that will facilitate your analysis (e.g., CHAT and CLAN), but this is rare and not available for RxTA.

After you have made all these decisions, you need to decide on whether you are going to type into a document that you can go straight into coding from, or whether you are going to transcribe first and format for coding later. If you want to code transcripts directly you might want large margins or even to type directly into tables with each line representing one turn in the conversation. If you want large margins you might want to have your page landscape rather than portrait. You might also want 1.5 or double spacing so there is more space to jot down thoughts. Even if you just want to get the words down and worry about formatting afterwards you will need to decide some shorthands such as R for researcher and P for participant to determine who is speaking, and what you are going to include and what you aren't, for example the 'ums' and 'ers', laughter, tears, sighs and pauses. Check out the key books on qualitative analysis in all the further reading sections (Chapters 13–15) for some ideas around these, but it is acceptable to develop your own method.

Now you have made the relevant decisions, you need to sit down and do it! I have known some transcription demons who can start at the beginning and just work through to the end. However, my own process doesn't work like that. When I first sit down I can usually concentrate for over an hour, sometimes two on a good day. Then I need to take a break and when I come back to it, I'll be lucky to get to an hour, often it is more like 45 minutes. However, when I come back to it after another break, I'm then lucky to get 20 minutes! This isn't how it is for everyone, but very soon you will know your own pattern. If it is like mine then you learn pretty quickly not to schedule transcription in for full days, but to schedule it with other tasks like writing or coding or contacting participants. You also learn pretty quickly not to give into the urge to get up and make coffee in the first hour or so as you won't get back into it. Try and learn your own pattern of what works and work with it rather than fighting it. Transcription takes hours per hour of interview, so you are going to be doing this for a long time!

When you get to the end, it is always worth auditing your transcriptions, or better still getting someone else to audit them. This ensures you haven't made too many mistakes or errors.

Analysis. How analysis is meant to go:

Figure 12.1 What the book says are the standard stages for thematic analysis

How analysis usually goes

Figure 12.2 What real-life thematic analysis looks like

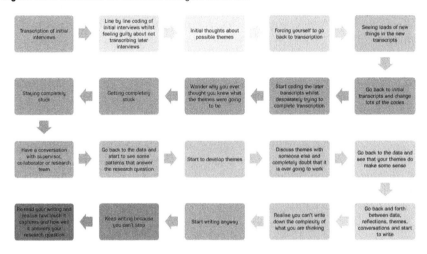

The analysis process involves art as well as science. You will be coding your transcriptions, developing themes, deciding on the themes you are going to write about, and writing about them as has been described in previous chapters. However, in RxTA, both the coding and development of themes involves interrogating your data for underlying meanings. Efforts to understand the meaning of your participants' words and experiences can lead to feelings of uncertainty and a wish to stay close to the words of your participants. However, this isn't the true nature of RxTA, which requires engagement with the data in a different way that allows access to the underlying meaning. Supervision and team work can be really helpful in working through these feelings as a researcher.

Write up: In the write up you need to consider both how to separate or combine your results and discussion sections, and also how to adhere to the COREQ guidelines (Booth et al. 2014). Braun and Clarke explain that the sense-making that occurs in the process of analysis does not happen in the absence of theory. Thus, as theory and the previous literature is core to our understanding of our data, it can make more sense to combine results and discussion. Although there are aspects of the COREQ guidelines that aren't applicable to RxTA (e.g., saturation – see Braun and Clarke 2019b), they can be helpful in identifying key aspects of your write up that should be present. Ideally you would be aware of these from the start of your writing, but even if you consider them late in the process, they can help you reflect on what you have and haven't included.

How does this method usually go wrong and what can you do about it?

The things that usually go wrong in RxTA are often to do with misunderstanding what RxTA is. Many people skim read the 2006 paper without consideration of the rich body of later writings. The main issue that arises in RxTA is that the analysis is not deep or thorough enough. This can result in topic or domain summaries being presented as themes. Read the relevant sections in the Understanding TA section of the Reflexive Thematic Analysis website (www.thematicanalysis.net) for more information on this. This issue can also result in you having too many themes or the analysis relying too much on quotes. There isn't a minimal or maximum number of themes or quotes that is appropriate for RxTA, but having a lot of them can often indicate that the analysis has stopped too early. Sometimes researchers, or reviewers, can be drawn to talking about saturation or counting the number of participants who contribute to each theme. This isn't appropriate in RxTA. Again, documents on the website will help you understand why this is, and also give you appropriate confidence to push back against reviewers who suggest you need them. Beyond this, reflexive thematic analysis is such a flexible approach that very little usually goes wrong.

What are the practical issues associated with this method?

Given its flexibility there are few practical issues in using reflexive TA. Most of the things that go wrong, as described in the section above, are conceptual rather than practical. You can deal with having heterogenous participants. You can deal with having a variety of types of data. You can deal with some interviews being 10 minutes and some being two hours. You can start your analysis before all the data is collected or you can wait until you have all your data.

Ethics

Most of the ethical issues involved in conducting RxTA are those involved in research in general and qualitative research specifically. These include informed consent, confidentiality, managing risk, anonymity, good management of data and protecting participants' rights. There may be additional considerations about the interpretation of data which are discussed in the ethics section in Chapter 15.

Example: Collecting rich data using a mix of interview techniques

Heffernan, M., Wilson, C., Keating, K. McCarthy, K., (2021). "Why Isn't It Going Away?": A Qualitative Exploration of Worry and Pain Experiences in Adolescents with Chronic Pain. *Pain Medicine*, 22(2), 459–469, https://doi.org/10.1093/pm/pnaa245

Marese was interested in young people in paediatric settings, especially those for whom there wasn't a specific diagnosis, either because there wasn't a diagnosis that could explain their symptoms or that the problem went beyond their symptoms. Pain was something that was common to many of these young people. A colleague involved in the pain management clinic in one of the local children's hospitals was also keen to support research on the topic. I was working on another study of worry and pain as they seemed to be so important to study together and the clinicians, and Marese herself, were interested in the experiences of the young people. Together we decided to explore the differing phenomenology of worry and pain to see what the commonalities and differences were. However, the clinicians on the team were also keen to know what the pain levels of the young people were and what their catastrophising was like. Catastrophising was considered to be an important construct in understanding the relationship between worry and pain and so we decided that we would use the questionnaires as a structure for getting our data. Marese planned an interview schedule with both open-ended questions, but also with the questionnaire questions included. This allowed us to characterise our participants in terms of their pain and catastrophising levels, while focusing on their experiences.

The choice of RxTA for our analysis was not difficult. We wanted to understand the meaning of our participants' experiences and look at psychological processes underlying both worry and pain, but we wanted these experiences to be varied, reflecting our collective clinical experience, rather than homogenous. These research aims, combined with our methods of collecting data, meant that RxTA was the best choice for our analysis.

Further reading

This approach has been developed by Braun and Clarke, so here are some of the most relevant books, chapters and papers.

Braun, V., & Clarke, V. (2006) Using thematic analysis in psychology. *Qualitative Research in Psychology*, 3(2), 77–101. DOI: https://doi.org/10.1191/1478088706qp063oa

Braun, V., & Clarke, V. (2013) *Successful Qualitative Research: A practical guide for beginners*. London: Sage.

Braun, V., & Clarke, V. (2019a) Reflecting on reflexive thematic analysis. *Qualitative Research in Sport, Exercise and Health*, 11(4), 589–597. DOI: https://doi.org/10.1080/2159676X.2019.1628806

Braun, V., & Clarke, V. (2019b) To saturate or not to saturate? Questioning data saturation as a useful concept for thematic analysis and sample-size rationales. *Qualitative Research in Sport, Exercise and Health*, 1–16. DOI: https://doi.org/10.1080/2159 676X.2019.1704846

Braun, V. & Clarke, V. (2022) *Thematic Analysis: A practical guide.* London: Sage.

Braun, V., Clarke, V. & Gray, D. (2017) *Collecting Qualitative Data: A practical guide to textual, media and virtual techniques.* Cambridge: Cambridge University Press.

Also check out https://www.thematicanalysis.net/ for everything RxTA!

Chapter reference

Booth, A., Hannes, K., Harden, A., Noyes, J., Harris, J., & Tong, A. (2014). COREQ (Consolidated Criteria for Reporting Qualitative Studies). In *Guidelines for Reporting Health Research: A User's Manual* (pp. 214–226). Chichester: John Wiley & Sons, Ltd. DOI: https://doi.org/10.1002/9781118715598.ch21

13 Grounded Theory

Humans, especially psychologists, are natural pattern observers, and indeed research can be seen as an endeavour to identify patterns, whether that be patterns in numerical data or patterns in people's experiences, or patterns in people's speech. There are lots of different ways of going about finding, measuring and describing those patterns, but sometimes we want to go beyond simple description to describe patterns in a way that can help us understand the relationships between them, and to make predictions about how different aspects of our lives and our experiences are related. Grounded theory was initially developed by Glaser and Strauss in order to bridge a gap between theory and empirical data. They saw theories being developed with an absence of a good understanding of a topic empirically. They felt that theories could be best developed from bottom-up observation and data, rather than finding empirical data to support top-down theories.

There are lots of examples of where this has been done, but perhaps without it being a formal grounded theory approach. I can't help thinking of the amazing work of Judy Dunn (1988) on young children's social lives, or even Aaron Tim Beck's (1979) systematic observations of the current concerns of his depressed clients that led to the very earliest development of cognitive behaviour therapy. What grounded theory as an approach does, however, is to give us a framework for systematically collecting data and analysing it in a way that helps us develop new theories.

What is this approach?

Grounded Theory is a qualitative research method designed to collect and analyse data to develop new theories. As described in Chapter 3, theories go beyond description with the aim of explaining phenomena and that may allow us to make predictions about how different constructs are related to each other and how this might impact us over time.

There are distinct versions of Grounded Theory. Glaser and Strauss initially developed it with the idea that the theories were there to be discovered, perhaps like gravity or other physical laws of nature. The guidelines they developed in their books was how to reveal these theories and what safeguards to put in place to ensure their reliability and validity. Over time this approach appeared to become too restrictive and not reflective of the reality of the development of theories, and Strauss worked with Corbin to further develop a new grounded theory approach.

The third approach, and the one I will focus on in this chapter, was further developed by Charmaz. Charmaz called her approach Constructivist Grounded

Theory to indicate its epistemology. Charmaz emphasised the constructed nature of knowledge when it came to understanding people, their experiences, and their relationships. With this shift away from empiricism also came a loosening of the 'rules' of Grounded Theory, and a more applicable approach that could be used in studies that could be done in a shorter time frame.

Grounded Theory uses qualitative data, collected through a variety of methods, including interviews, researcher memoing, meetings and observations, and analyses this data with a focus on relationships between the different constructs that are important in the data. The end point is a theory that has modes, or themes, that describe key features of the theory, with rich description of how they are related.

Philosophy

Different approaches to Grounded Theory have different philosophies. Glaser subscribed to a very empiricist view of research, seeing Grounded Theory as the bridge between theory and empirical data. Charmaz on the other hand was very much a constructivist, seeing the factors that we usually are interested in as being constructed by our own narratives and in the relationship between the researcher and their participants. That does mean that you can use Grounded Theory more flexibly to fit the epistemology that fits with your own understanding of your topic and with the question you are asking. However, that also entails thinking about it. Unlike an experimental study or an Interpretative Phenomenological Analysis that have a set epistemology, Grounded Theory requires you to determine how you are interpreting the meaning of your data and to work out what truth claims you are making.

What kind of questions are best answered using this method?

Grounded Theory tends to attract people who want to go beyond a description of people's experiences to a theory of them. You will probably be interested in how different aspects of the person's experience work together and you may be more interested in processes than topics. Questions are likely to be phrased in terms of 'How can we best understand…?'. If you are unsure whether Grounded Theory is a good fit for your question check out Box 13.1.

What are the key steps to using this method?

Grounded Theory has perhaps the least fixed methodology of the qualitative approaches as you follow your developing theory as you develop it. Therefore, although the steps below are in a particular order, there is a lot of going round in loops in these steps.

The first step in grounded theory is to **determine what your question is**. Different versions of Grounded Theory determine different approaches to working on this. Glaser was quite clear that you shouldn't have pre-conceptions, and therefore you shouldn't read the literature before starting. However, there are a few problems with this. One problem is that we risk re-inventing the wheel and devise a theory about something that already has good theories or empirical work underpinning our understanding of it. If there has already been a lot of empirical work, then maybe a narrative synthesis of this might be more helpful than a new study. If there is an existing theory, then maybe further testing of this might be more helpful. The second problem occurs when you are completing this work for a qualification. In this case you do not have unlimited time, and often the supervisor and the institution want to see progress in understanding the existing literature in appraisals of your progress. You may even need to submit a literature review prior to starting the data collection phase at all. The final problem, and perhaps the one that is most salient in applied psychological research is that most people choose their topic because they have an interest in it. This might be a personal interest, a professional interest, or an interest borne out of reading about a topic. In all these cases, not understanding what is already known about a topic risks us enhancing our own biases about a topic. Glaser put all different kinds of checks and balances into his approach to Grounded Theory to mitigate this risk, but this adds time, complexity, and isn't always possible within the timeframe of many research projects.

Therefore, I recommend having some understanding of the literature about your topic. This can help you overcome your own biases, but also can help you boundary the question. What I mean by this is that a theory of something vast, such as shame or dignity, might be beyond the scope of many applied researchers. However, if you put some boundaries around this, such as shame in the context of sending your child to childcare, or dignity in the context of physical disability and public transport, then this might be a topic that you can develop a theory of in a reasonable time. These boundaries are best developed in conversations, with a research team, and if you can, with participant representatives.

Once you have your research question with appropriate boundaries, you need to **design a data collection strategy**. Participants are important, but they come after the data collection strategy. In Grounded Theory all is data. You are not bound by simply doing interviews with participants. You can ask them to complete measures or surveys, take part in focus groups, and take part in interviews. You can observe meetings between your participants and others (with proper consent), you can include what other people have written about your topic, and you can include your own responses and reflections. Remember, you are trying to develop a theory that fits the most amount of data, and therefore wherever the data comes from you need your theory to be able to explain it. Your data collection strategy can evolve across the course of your study, but you need to start somewhere. Often this will involve interviews or focus groups with key participants. One of the unique features of Grounded Theory is the changing nature of your interview questions as you go through data collection and theory development. Therefore, at this stage you want indicative questions, and an indicative process of data collection.

Identify your participants. In a Grounded Theory study this will be an ongoing process as you start to develop your theory and start to look for people who may be able to talk to exceptions in your theory. At the start however, you are likely to be looking for a wide range of participants. This might encompass variety in the demographics of your participants, such as age, gender, ethnicity, sexuality, disability status, marital and relationship status, but it might also encompass variety in the experience of the phenomena you are researching. For example, if you are developing a theory of change in an intervention you are likely to want participants who responded well to the intervention, those who did badly, those who didn't complete the intervention, and those who thought it was fine, but didn't particularly benefit. See the example below for a discussion of this in action. It is worth thinking about this in advance, especially how you are going to encourage those people who maybe won't want to engage with research on the topic, as these people are crucial to the development of your theory. In Grounded Theory you are going to work very closely with your participant gatekeepers so conversations with them should start early and be regular.

The data collection, coding, theorising, data collection cycle. This is where the fun starts. You will start data collection, whether that is doing the first few interviews, or a focus group, or observations of your participants, and then you will start the theorising work. You will transcribe the data, start the coding (see the following section on coding and Box 13.2), and start to identify what you need more information on. Until you have a few interviews or focus groups done you are unlikely to want to change your interview protocol much, but by listening back to your interviews and thinking about what else you need to know you will be able to better tune in to your next participants. As you go through this repeated process you will start to identify what you want to ask more about, and which participant voices are not currently being represented. This process is exciting, and it can feel very liberating, but this freedom can also feel scary, especially for someone starting out in research or in Grounded Theory. I often get questions like 'what if this is the wrong theory and I am going to miss something if I change participants or questions?'. This is a great question and there are two answers. The first is that if you are early in the process, then keep it broad. Keep recruiting participants and keep asking all your questions. If it isn't coming together then keep it broad and keep going back to your research question and your data. The second answer is a question! What is your GT approach and what is your epistemology? If you are completing a Glaserian Grounded Theory study, then you clearly don't have enough data – the theory should become clearer with more data. If you are completing a Charmazian Grounded Theory study, then it is *your* theory and if you are using all the coding strategies you can then it can't be wrong, just sloppy and poor quality. Use your tools and the process will work.

Box 13.1: Aligning the question with the method

Research question	Qualitative or quantitative	Why
What are young people's experiences of using public transport?	Qualitative	The focus is on the experience, and there are no hypotheses indicated in the question
What do people with heart disease think about changing medications?	Qualitative	The question is exploratory with no assumptions about what might be found
What meaning do barristers make of defending people who they think are guilty?	Qualitative	Qualitative research is great at focusing on meaning, in a way that quantitative studies can't
Are young people better at working technology than older people?	Quantitative	There is a clear hypothesis in the question. This question cannot be fully answered by an exploration of people's experiences
What are the stress levels of dental technicians?	Quantitative	Level of stress can, and therefore probably should, be measured quantitatively
What is a nurse's role in palliative care?	Quantitative	This is not a quantitative question at first sight, but a quick reading of the literature suggests that there are a lot of qualitative studies about this. Unless you are working in a particularly unique context, another qualitative study might not add anything
What worries do children and adolescents have following the COVID-19 pandemic?	Either or mixed	We know quite a lot about what things worry children, but we might miss some of these in the COVID-19 context. Therefore, it might be helpful to explore with open-ended questions. However, it might also be helpful to have questionnaires about worries or to quantify the answers to the open-ended questions

Research question	Qualitative or quantitative	Why
What experiences lead to drop-out from university medical training?	Either or mixed	As above, we know some of the factors that cause drop-out from university, but few studies focus on drop-out from medical training, as it is rare. We could ask open-ended questions to get a good selection of experiences, but it might be helpful to quantify these or to add questionnaires about drop-out into the study
How can we best understand the role of alexithymia in autistic burnout?	Either	This question begs the development or testing of a model. Therefore, grounded theory or model testing seem best. It might be possible to develop a mixed methods study, especially sequential mixed methods, but for a single study one approach might be best

This step only finishes when you have a well-developed theory based firmly in your data that has explicitly sought out exceptions, both in terms of your participants and in terms of your processes identified.

Coding

'Coding is the pivotal link between collecting data and developing an emergent theory to explain these data. Through coding, you define what is happening in the data and begin to grapple with what it means." Charmaz (2014), p113.

Initial coding is where the transcripts are read carefully, word-by-word or line-by-line or incident-by-incident and words noted that capture the meaning of the word/sentence or incident.

As you read through your transcript you want to make notes on what you are reading that stay close to the text but focus on processes. Sometimes this is called coding for gerunds. Gerunds are action or doing words – 'ing' words if you like. By coding for gerunds, you are constantly challenging yourself to see the processes involved in your data rather than the topics. This is crucial if you are developing a theory.

Focused coding is the first part of analytic coding. Some initial codes are developed based on their importance in answering the research question. Their meaning is interrogated across the dataset. Charmaz (2014) asks the question 'What kinds of theoretical categories do these codes indicate?' (p144), but I would also ask 'How do these codes help me answer my research question?'.

Focused coding starts by identifying key codes. These might be the most frequent or important codes from your initial coding; they might be ones that combine a range of initial codes into a meaningful new code. With each key code you identify or develop, you interrogate it with respect to the meaning it holds in relation to your data. This will often mean writing memos (see Box 13.3) about what the code means to you and then going back to the data to check whether it captures the meaning of the data given what your interpretation of it is. As you develop different focused codes, you compare what they mean in relation to each other – are they part of a process, or do they relate to the same process, but are different aspects of it? It is in the process of going between your initial codes, your focused codes, your data and your memos that you will start to develop the process of constant comparison.

Box 13.2: Coding

People often have their own ways of coding that can seem crazy to others. You may want to use specific qualitative research software such as NVivo or MAXQDA and that might be what makes most sense to you. However, you don't have to use coding software in order to do everything electronically. You can use a word processing programme, with highlighting, comments, large margins, etc. The great thing about word processing packages is that it is possible to search the whole document for specific phrases. This can be helpful to find additional examples of something, or just when you remember that a participant said something, and you want to find it quickly. Another benefit of this approach is that it is easy to create your audit trail. An audit trail is evidence of your research decisions. Inter-rater reliability isn't important in most qualitative research, but being able to stand over your research decisions and being able to document your thinking throughout the whole process is important. Koch (1994) argues that with an audit trail a different researcher could come up with a similar analysis and would not come up with a contradictory analysis. If you have everything on the computer, then this is relatively easy.

Some people, however, including myself, find the process of coding a very physical one. I tend to print out my transcripts, have lots of pens and highlighters as I go through them. I highlight important phrases and words, I scribble thoughts on transcripts, and I tend to use the computer to write up reflections and memos. I try not to overthink the process and use colours freely and then afterwards try to reflect on what those colours mean. The process must be systematic, and I do go through all the coding processes, but I do them with colour, and freely. Once I have done this, I can gather colours together, review what I have highlighted, read my scribbles and repeat the process to bring the codes together for themes. At this stage I might employ the post-its, again in different colours. I can write codes on them and see where they are in the transcripts, I can write further memos on them, and I can start to develop themes on them. A different approach is to find the sentences that pertain to each code and to cut them out of the transcripts and arrange these cut outs physically. This always reminds me of table planning for an event such as a wedding – you know already that some people must sit together, and some people absolutely can't, but you don't know what the best arrangement is. By cutting the quotes out you can keep re-arranging them and putting them at different 'tables', all the time reflecting on whether a particular arrangement works well, works badly, and whether it is surprising or comfortable.

These physical approaches seem to allow creativity in the process more easily but have the disadvantage that it is easy to lose evidence of your decisions and therefore you can end up with an incomplete audit trail.

There isn't a right or wrong way of how you go about coding your data, you will hopefully find a way that suits you. Talk to others around you who have completed qualitative analysis and see what different approaches they have taken. Steal the best ideas from them and find your own unique way. You are still going to be taking a systematic approach, using a reflective diary and/or memos, creating an audit trail, as well as using any of the techniques specific to a qualitative technique such as constant comparison (GT) or coding for language and content (IPA), but the actual physical process of coding will be different.

Axial coding, developed by Corbin, doesn't happen in all types of Grounded Theory. It refers to development of each code along its axes or properties and dimensions. That means thinking about the code in terms of 'when, where, why, who, how and with what consequences' (Strauss and Corbin, 1998, p125).

Axial coding involves sorting the data, synthesising it and then organising it into categories/themes that bring lots of data together coherently. By asking of your focused codes what do you know about them in terms of their key dimensions, and by memoing as you do this, you can determine the edges of your codes, perhaps who next to interview, and can start to map out how your codes and categories relate to each other. Axial coding supplies a framework for examining your data systematically and provides a window into being more analytic. However, it is not necessary (nor sufficient) to do this.

Theoretical coding, developed by Glaser, involves further development of the focused codes either using theory or further analysis and constant comparison (see Box 13.3). This also isn't used in every version of grounded theory.

Theoretical coding involves further development of your focused codes. It can involve integration of existing theory or codes that originate in your discipline, but it can involve developing more analytical codes that move the codes and the relationships between them to a more theoretical understanding. Just like axial coding, theoretical coding involves systematically examining the data and determining the parameters or properties of the codes. Unlike axial coding, theoretical coding moves towards the development of the theory. In practice this involves examining carefully your focused codes and memoing the theoretical aspects of them. This might involve reflecting on what theories they remind you of, or why they are different to existing theories. When you are happy with the name of your code, and you think you understand what the code is doing, then you go back to the data to check to see whether the code does make sense across the dataset, and whether you have its parameters right. You might want to combine codes or separate them.

Constructing a theory. Not all versions of Grounded Theory require a theory to be developed. If you do construct a theory, then you put together your focused or theoretical codes in a way that is supported by your data and in a way that shows how they are related to each other in time and/or space. The philosophy chosen for the overall study should inform your view of what a theory is and therefore what your theory aims to do. A positivist approach to grounded theory will require the development of a theory which explains, perhaps predicts, and that focuses on generalisability and universality. In contrast, a constructionist approach to grounded theory will require a theory that understands how participants have constructed meaning of their experiences. It allows multiple realities, indeterminacy and a focus on processes as they are experienced, rather than the focus being on how well they predict and explain.

In developing your theory you go through your codes and start to systematically examine the relationships between them. These might be temporal relationships, or systemic relationships. You might want to think about the direction(s) of influence between them. You might want one code to be completely contained by another. Even at this stage you might combine codes or separate them, and you will still be going back to your data constantly to check that your theory represents the meaning of it well.

This stage often involves lots of scribbling on paper and trying out different ways of understanding the relationships between the codes you have developed to see which is a best representation of your data.

Box 13.3: Processes involved in Grounded Theory

Process	What is it?	How to do it
Memoing	Memoing is a way of systematically reflecting on and analysing your data that takes it from a surface understanding to a deeper analytical understanding.	Memoing involves writing notes about your thoughts and reflections on some aspect of your analysis. This includes exploring your initial beliefs about your focused or theoretical codes and reflecting on specific interviews. The aim is to develop a more analytical, more interpretative understanding of your data and of your own preconceptions of what your data and what your codes mean.
Constant comparison	Constant comparison is a method of ensuring quality in grounded theory studies. It helps you sort and organise your data, and your codes in a structured way that facilitates the development of a new theory.	In practice, constant comparison involves comparing your initial codes with your data to determine that the codes represent something real in the data. It involves comparing different initial codes to determine whether and how they are related, whether they are independent of each other, and whether they represent independent data points. Finally, constant comparison means comparing your final theory with your codes and with your data to ensure that you can map them onto each other.
Saturation	The concept of saturation is that the data collection and analysis continue until no new codes emerge. It has been widely critiqued; with many researchers contesting that experience is too nuanced to fully saturate any analysis.	In principle, saturation is continuing your data collection and analysis until there is nothing else to know about your theory. However, this could lead to collecting additional data, or it could mean doing additional analysis. When you are interrogating your codes for their boundaries or their theoretical relevance, then you are determining whether you know everything you need to know about them. I think what most people mean when they say they analysed their data until saturation was achieved is that no new codes were emerging, but in grounded theory, saturation means more than that.

Finalising your theory. When you have a well-developed theory, you need to finalise the theory. This involves drawing up your theory, usually visually, doing final checks that you have evidence for all parts of the theory, and finding quotes to illustrate the theory.

How does this method usually go wrong and what you can do about it?

There are two main ways in which this method goes wrong; you can't recruit participants who will provide an alternative account of the phenomenon of interest, such as those who have had negative experiences or who have had unusual experiences, or you run out of time and can't complete the analysis sufficiently to develop your theory fully.

The first problem can be minimised, although not eliminated, by careful planning and working closely with your gatekeepers. It is worth asking questions such as 'have I got permission to contact people who are no longer in the service?' and 'who are the people who haven't done so well, and what happens to them?'. You will have to be clear with these gatekeepers about how important these participants are to your study, as some gatekeepers may be reluctant to approach them. It may be that you need alternative pathways to recruit these participants, such as more public or social media adverts or through voluntary organisations. The other part of solving this problem is time-management. You may well not know which participants you are missing until you are quite far into the recruitment process, and so you need time to find these participants and find ways of making it attractive for them to take part.

The second problem is harder because time-management of projects is often the hardest part. As Hugh Kearns states in his brilliant book, *Time for Research: Time management for academics, researchers and PhD students* (2006), plan how long it will take and triple it! As recruitment takes up so much time, especially if you are transcribing and coding in between participants, then it is easy to not leave enough time to properly develop the final theory. However, forewarned is forearmed, and so planning sufficient time at the end of the project for this important part is crucial. This stage also benefits from not having to do it alone. Talk to your research team, talk to colleagues (without breaking confidentiality), talk to anyone who will listen about your developing theory and use these conversations to reflect on your own understandings of your theory, and to develop it further.

What are the practical issues associated with this method?

The practical issues are those things that go wrong in grounded theory and so are addressed in the previous section.

Ethics

As well as the usual issues involved in research such as confidentiality, managing risk, participant rights and keeping your data safely, the big ethical issue in grounded theory is informed consent. This is unique to grounded theory because your procedure might change as the project progresses, so all those sentences on the consent form about what your participants are going to be asked to do have to be general enough that you don't constantly have to change your forms. Of course, a consent form and information sheet don't have to be the only aspect of consent, they are the minimum, and it is often quite easy to add details about the procedure when you are talking to potential participants. It is unlikely that your project will change so much that general sentences about the topic of the project and about what your participants will be asked to do will become misleading, but it is worth designing these two documents with this in mind. The other side to this is that ethics committees often want to see an interview schedule with your application, and you will have to be honest about what the schedule is, in that it is indicative of the questions asked, rather than exactly what will be asked. Some ethics committees deal very well with this, and a few quotes from Grounded Theory texts can help ethics committee members to feel confident in this process, but some committees take a little more convincing and you may have to give examples of how the schedule might change over time, or in the worst-case scenario, you may have to check in with the committee each time your interview changes.

Example: Developing a theory and the importance of exceptions

Conlon, C. M., Wilson, C. E., Gaffney, P. & Stoker, M. (2018). Wilderness therapy intervention with adolescents: Exploring the process of change, *Journal of Adventure Education and Outdoor Learning*, 18:4, 353–366, DOI: 10.1080/14729679.2018.1474118

Claire was working with colleagues who were trying out a new approach to working with the most disengaged young people in the system. These young people were all at risk of being excluded from their home. Many had been in the justice system, and many had mental health or addiction problems. The clinicians working on the wilderness programme were amazed at how engaged these young people were on the programme and they were seeing some clear changes. However, it wasn't clear to them what aspects of the programme were making the most difference. Different clinicians pinpointed different things, all of which could be supported by existing literature, but it wasn't clear how they worked together.

It seemed that if we were to try and make sense of the mechanisms of change, especially if we wanted to see how different mechanisms worked with each other, then Grounded Theory was the best approach. Glaser's approach to

Grounded Theory didn't work for us; it was too restrictive and made too many assumptions that didn't fit. There were aspects of Strauss' Grounded Theory approach that did work, but the approach that fit our shared assumptions best was Charmaz's (2008, 2014) Constructionist Grounded Theory.

Claire started by interviewing a few young people who had thoroughly enjoyed the wilderness programme and who were delighted to talk about it. Claire transcribed these interviews and coded them, and we started talking about emerging findings. Just as predicted, several different processes seemed to be important for the young people, but we were aware that we had a very similar set of participants at this stage. Claire and I chatted about what kinds of participants we needed to help 'test' the developing model. Most of the participants were male, so we wondered about trying to recruit female participants. The initial participants had all attended the programme at the same time, so we wondered about recruiting participants from other groups. However, most importantly we decided that we needed to recruit participants who had not had such a good time. Only by looking for the exceptions could we truly see whether our developing model was a good one. Claire went back to the clinicians running the programme and we asked them to help us recruit people who had not had such a good experience. This can be a tricky thing to ask because it can feel like a criticism of the clinicians. We were lucky in that they were very open to our request. Only one participant who had not had a good experience of the programme agreed to take part, but they were crucial to our final model.

Further reading

Books

Glaser, B. G., & Strauss, A. L. (2017) *The Discovery of Grounded Theory: Strategies for qualitative research.* London: Routledge.
This is the most recent Glaser book on his version of grounded theory.

Strauss, A., & Corbin, J. M. (1998) *Grounded Theory in Practice.* Thousand Oaks, CA: Sage.
This is the key text for Strauss's version of grounded theory.

Charmaz, K. (2014) *Constructing Grounded Theory.* London: Sage.
Charmaz takes a different approach, and this is developed well in this book.

Charmaz, K. (2008). Reconstructing grounded theory. *The SAGE Handbook of Social Research Methods,* 461–478. London: Sage.
This chapter might be an alternative introduction to Charmaz's approach.

Pidgeon, N., & Henwood, K. (2004) Grounded theory. In Bryman and Hardy, *Handbook of Data Analysis* (pp. 625–648). London: Sage.
An accessible chapter from independent researchers.

Chapter references

Beck, A. T. (ed.). (1979). *Cognitive Therapy of Depression.* New York: Guilford press.

Dunn, J. (1988). *The Beginnings of Social Understanding.* Cambridge, MA: Harvard University Press.

Kearns, H. & Gardiner, M. (2006). *Time for Research: Time management for PhD students.* Adelaide, SA: Flinders University – Staff Development and Training Unit.

Koch, T. (1994). Establishing rigour in qualitative research: The decision trail. *Journal of Advanced Nursing, 19*(5), 976–986. DOI: https://doi.org/10.1111/j.1365-2648.1994.tb01177.x

14 Interpretative phenomenological analysis (IPA)

What is this approach?

Interpretative Phenomenological Analysis, or IPA, is a qualitative research approach that uses interpretation (or hermeneutics) to make sense of people's lived experience (phenomenology). It prioritises the individual experience (idiography) while looking for commonalities across a few people with homogenous experiences. The focus is on the meaning participants hold about their experiences. It has gained in popularity within applied psychological research with the writings of Jonathan Smith and his colleagues.

Philosophy

The philosophy of IPA is perhaps the most written about compared to the other qualitative approaches in this book. This is perhaps because some of the key aspects of IPA – its hermeneutic approach, its roots in phenomenology and its idiographic focus, are all rooted in philosophy. See Box 14.1.

What kind of questions are best answered using this method?

IPA is most often chosen when the researcher is interested in participant experiences. It works well when the focus is on the participants' meaning-making in relation to their experiences, and when the experiences are important to the participants so that they have reflections on their experiences. IPA is often chosen when the researcher wants to focus on a small number of participants, and when they have access to this number of homogenous participants.

What are the key steps in using this method?

Find the question: The choice of IPA should be guided by the research question being best answered using this approach. Lots of applied researchers are interested in their participants' lived experiences, but it is worth knowing a bit more about IPA, what it does do, and what it doesn't do, before deciding that IPA is the best way of answering a question about lived experience. Other qualitative research approaches might also be able to answer these questions without having to focus on meaning, interpretation, and idiographic details. See Smith, Flowers and Larkin (2021) p42 for great examples of good IPA questions.

Box 14.1: Philosophical underpinnings of IPA

	What it means	How it applies to IPA
Hermeneutics/ Interpretation Read Heidegger	Hermeneutics is concerned with interpretation. Its early origins are in the interpretation of religious texts in order to uncover their true meaning, but hermeneutics in relation to psychology is interested in verbal and non-verbal behaviour. Interpretation of words, whether written or spoken, is designed to uncover the meaning of those words.	In IPA the hermeneutic is demonstrated with the participant making sense of the meaning of their experiences in the research process. Smith talks about a double hermeneutic where the researcher then makes sense of the participant's sense-making. As the aim of IPA is to uncover meanings, interpretation is crucial to finding those meanings. IPA contends that the underlying meaning is accessible by interpretation of people's accounts of their experiences in conjunction with awareness of their own pre-existing knowledge and biases that could impact the researcher's meaning-making. In IPA the researcher brackets their own experience off from their analysis of the texts.
Phenomenology Read Husserl, Merleau-Ponty	Phenomenology is an approach to knowledge. Phenomenology values knowledge created by exploration of our own experiences. In phenomenology, our conscious experience of life is the focus of the development of understanding and knowledge.	IPA research creates new knowledge by examining people's conscious experiences of important aspects of their lives. While Husserl proposed that phenomenology should focus on uncovering and describing the essence of a phenomenon, IPA as used in psychology research proposes that we should attend to the detail of individuals' experiences.

	What It means	How it applies to IPA
Idiography Read Allport, Windelband	Something idiographic is something that relates to the individual and can be contrasted with the nomothetic, which relates to general laws/understandings.	IPA privileges individual experiences. When analysing the experiences of several participants, IPA asks that you treat each one as an individual first and do your analysis per person before looking for commonalities across participants' experiences. Because of this, IPA often calls for homogeneity of participants so that the commonalities are meaningful.

Design the interview and practice: In order to achieve a double hermeneutic in an IPA interview, the questions and the interviewer need to get underneath a surface recall of experience to a deeper level. An interview schedule should guide questioning without restricting it, indeed IPA researchers have been advised to devise the interview schedule, get familiar with it, know all the questions and why they are there, and then to ignore it all and stay with the participant while they recount their experiences, showing empathic curiosity about these. There is more detailed advice in Chapter 4 of Smith et al. (2021).

Find suitable participants: As mentioned above, you will need homogenous participants for a good IPA study. This either means advertising for/approaching only the participants who fit your criteria, or by casting the net wider and then choosing the ones that best answer your research question (see below for a discussion of the ethics of this). If you are working through gatekeepers, this might mean ongoing conversations with them about who is and isn't suitable. When your gatekeepers know your participants well, and they only need to approach a small number of them, they may well approach ones that they think are suitable, such as the ones they think will take part, or ones that have good things to say about a service. This is great when these are the people you want to take part, but your agenda and that of your gatekeepers might not be the same!

Collect the data: For an IPA study, this usually involves individual interviews as these offer the opportunity for meaning-making to take place for an individual. There are examples of IPA being done using focus groups and meaning making in focus groups certainly occurs but perhaps in a different way. Most research studies collect data from a participant in one meeting, but there are no hard-and-fast rules about this, and to develop the double hermeneutic more than one interview per participant might be helpful. As is true for all qualitative research, it is always worth listening back to your interview after it is completed, prior to doing the next interview. This alerts you to the times you didn't stay with the participant's experience, or you didn't go the step further to increase meaning-making. At this stage in an IPA study, you aren't going to change the interview (unlike during a grounded theory study), but you can help yourself improve the interview process.

Transcribe your interviews: When you can, the last step of collecting your data and the first step of analysing it is transcription. General guidelines about transcription can be found in Chapter 13. For IPA there are a few additional issues to consider. As you are interested in the meaning that your participants are making of their experiences, you might want to annotate your transcripts with comments on tone, on non-verbal communications (even on an audio-recording you might hear participants sigh or laugh or get louder or quieter) or on what was happening in the room during that interview. You might want to set out your transcripts ready for coding with room for comments on content, semantics and meaning.

Analyse your data: Analysis is always written about in stages and as if one stage follows the one before. However, researchers, including Smith and colleagues, readily acknowledge that it isn't linear. Analysis is iterative and you will move through the following stages back and forth several times.

Code for content, semantics and meaning across the full transcript. This involves a line-by-line analysis of 'the experiential claims,[1] concerns and understandings of each participant' (Smith et al. 2021, p.75).

Find patterns that draw together these codes. The patterns should emphasise convergence and divergence, even within individual participant experiences. The patterns, or personal experiential themes, should be meaningful and nuanced.

Look for commonalities across the different participant transcripts, codes and themes, again paying attention to divergence and convergence, nuance and meaning. These are likely to become group experiential themes.

Develop these commonalities further by having a dialogue between yourself, the data and wider knowledge and understanding (theory, clinical knowledge, etc.). This is where interpretation can make the understanding richer and deeper. Also, although you can have this dialogue yourself, it might also be helpful to have this dialogue with others to help you reflect on your own positionality and biases.

Develop a structure or framework that brings the themes together. It is all too common for the biggest or most important theme to come first and the smallest or least important theme to come last in the write up. This doesn't represent the gestalt of the data and so understanding how the themes fit together is crucial.

Organise your material and start writing. Writing is part of the analytic process and what you write does not have to be in your final research report. I often have at least three levels of writing open at one time: writing for the final

---

[1] 'Experiential claims' used to be called emergent themes, but this has been changed in recent writing about IPA as it is a better term for what it is.

report, writing for the purpose of developing my ideas, and writing for imme-
diate reflections and concerns. When you are writing for the final report you
are thinking about the reader, and you often put pressure on yourself to write
well, coherently and only write about the things you are sure about. If you free
yourself up to write more freely then new ideas emerge and, in the end, you
often end up writing well enough for it to be used in the final report.

Develop a full narrative of your results. This includes a detailed account
of the themes with quotes to evidence them and a commentary on these data
extracts. It may or may not include a visual guide. Box 14.2 highlights some
features of IPA you need to pay attention to in your narrative in order to demon-
strate excellence.

How does this method usually go wrong and what can we do about it?

Homogeneity of participants: Sometimes it is hard to recruit sufficient participants with exactly the profile you want. It might be that you have sufficient
people with type one diabetes attending your clinic, but that not enough of them
have poorly controlled diabetes for you to run your study. If you are struggling
to recruit, then it is tempting to widen your criteria. However, as participant
characteristics are important in IPA, it is worth making careful decisions about
what aspects of your criteria you want to widen. If you go back and interrogate
your research question you might find that you need people with poorly controlled diabetes, but that you could include participants with type two diabetes.
Recruitment of suitable participants also depends on why you are doing the
study. If you are completing a study as part of a qualification then there may be
requirements about how big the study is, but if you are doing it as a practitioner
it might be fine to have a smaller sample size.

Interviews stay on the surface: It rarely happens in an IPA study, but sometimes it is hard to get underneath the surface of what your participant is telling
you what. It could be that they are telling you about something that they have
rehearsed many times before in other settings. It could be that they are telling
you what they think you want to hear because they know they will see you in
the service after the research is over. It could be that they do not want to share
their deeper emotions or thoughts due to them being painful or shameful or
both. It *isn't* the researcher's job to distress participants, and you should always
be considerate of what participants want to share and what they do not, but it
is the researcher's job to be curious and ask questions that encourage participants to reflect on their experiences, not just to describe them. This process
is what uncovers the meaning. In order to overcome this problem, you first
need to identify that it is happening and then to hypothesise about why it is
happening. As a researcher are you very concerned about upsetting your participants at all? Are you worried about your own ability to contain participants'
emotions should they get very emotional? Are you ambivalent about your own

role as a researcher, because it feels so different to your usual helping role as a practitioner? Supervision and working in teams can be very helpful to identify any of our own barriers to creating meaning with our participants and working through them. Listening back to interviews and identifying where you might have deepened the exploration and identifying where it was appropriate not to can be helpful. It is also worth keeping in mind that across your participants' accounts of their experiences there will be individual differences in how reflective they are and having one interview which appears to stay on the surface is not a problem for most research projects!

Analysis isn't interpretative enough or deep enough: In any interpretative qualitative research there is a risk that the researcher gets pulled into summarising and describing their data, rather than interpreting it. This can happen because going from individual codes and using these to look for patterns across the dataset can pull you into trying to incorporate all the codes you have. It can happen because you value the time and experience of your participants and it feels wrong to leave anything out, even if it doesn't answer the research question, or is peripheral to the main findings. The other process that often happens is that researchers who have been exposed mostly to quantitative research find the subjectivity of qualitative research hard to sit with. They often have been drilled in issues such as validity and reliability, whether of measures or of procedures, and the myth of objectivity of quantitative research has been widely promoted. Even those researchers who value qualitative research can question their own interpretations of the data and even question whether they are right to interpret the data. Two main strategies are helpful here. One is going back to the method to check your own understanding of it. Going back to reading about hermeneutics and where the origins of interpretation of data comes from can be helpful to ground you in what you are trying to do. Reading about IPA (or other interpretative qualitative approaches) and reading good quality IPA studies can help orient you to what you are making claims about and what you are not. The second comes back to supervision and teamwork. Interpretation of qualitative data is mostly done individually but talking with a team or trusted colleague can identify whether you are staying too close to a descriptive account or whether you are making up crazy ideas about your data. Conversations can help you develop ideas about what your participants' meanings are, and then you go can back to the data to ensure that you can evidence your interpretations. In my experience, some of this just comes with doing it!

Working with your own biases: Bracketing of personal experiences is hard. Even for the most reflective practitioner there are things you are aware of believing, there are things you know you experienced in a particular way that you know have influenced you, and there are your fundamental ways of seeing the world that you have probably reflected on. However, there are two challenges inherent in bracketing off personal experience; the first is how to do it for the things you are aware of, and the second is how to become more aware of the things you aren't aware of! There are several different ways of being reflexive within an IPA analysis. Writing a reflective journal or reflective notes as you go along can be helpful to highlight what your initial responses are. Using this space for free writing following initial reflections can be helpful to get to a deeper understanding of where your reflections originate. In my experience, examiners (but not journal reviewers) often want to know how you used such a journal in your analysis and it is a good question. Do you go back to the reflective journal regularly to check out how you were thinking and feeling along the whole journey of the research? Do you read it at the end of each stage of analysis, e.g., after initial coding, after initial theme development, etc.? Do you read it at the end of the coding of each participant? And if you do, what do you do with your learning at each of these stages. What we would hope is that by comparing the data and your analysis of it to your initial reflections you become more aware of any biases that are influencing the analysis, or metaphorically, any lenses through which you are seeing the data. This doesn't have to be a solitary activity either. Working with your research team, including a supervisor if relevant, can help to identify biases within the team, including your own. Then the data can be interrogated with this understanding. One of the benefits of working with a research team is that you will have different biases and so will be better able to identify each other's biases. This of course requires good relationships in the team, trust between team members, and an acknowledgement of the power imbalances in any research team.

Dealing with biases you are unaware of is understandably harder as you don't know what you don't know. Even for the most reflective practitioner it is hard to develop increased awareness of things you don't even know are a belief or position, for example, the things you take for granted as a psychologist that a different social scientist wouldn't. Working with a diverse research group can also help and participant involvement can highlight the insider perspective if you are an outsider. The main strategy for dealing with these biases is being open to them.

Box 14.2: Four criteria for assessing excellent IPA (from Smith, Flowers, & Larkin, 2021).

Criteria	What it means	How it relates to underlying philosophy of IPA
'Constructing a compelling, unfolding narrative'	'The analysis tells a persuasive and coherent story. The narrative is built cumulatively through an unfolding analytic dialogue through carefully selected and interpreted extracts from participants.'	The construction of the narrative combines all three philosophical principles of IPA. Only by taking an idiographic perspective and understanding each participant, interpreting the participants' words to get at the underlying meaning, and being interested in something important to the participants allows you to create the narrative that is compelling. It also requires additional skills in writing.

Criteria	What it means	How it relates to underlying philosophy of IPA
'Developing a vigorous experiential and/or existential account'	'Focus on the important and/or existential meaning of participants' accounts gives depth to the analysis.'	This aspect of quality speaks to phenomenology. By focusing on what is important to participants you undertake a phenomenological endeavour.
'Close analytic reading of participants' words'	'Thorough analysis and interpretation of quoted material within the narrative helps give meaning to the data and the experience it describes.'	Interpretation is core to hermeneutics.
'Attending to convergence and divergence'	'Idiographic depth and systematic comparison between participants creates a dynamic interweaving of patterns of similarity and individual idiosyncrasy.'	By focusing on the individual and highlighting similarities and differences between individuals, the researcher is demonstrating their commitment to idiography.

If you can remain open to the fact you hold biases and commit to working with them, then when opportunities arise to challenge yourself, you will take them.

What are the practical issues associated with this method?

The practical issues associated with IPA are common to most qualitative approaches: equipment and technology, time and commitment to the process, and issues in coding. These are described in other chapters.

Ethics

Most of the ethical issues within an IPA study are the ones you would expect from doing qualitative research, namely the standard ethical issues of informed consent, confidentiality, and managing risk, with the ethical issues that are more pronounced in qualitative research, namely, anonymity and anonymising the data, and keeping your data safe (given that you are likely to have recordings as well as written transcripts). However, there are two additional issues that are worth consideration when doing an IPA study.

Choosing/rejecting participants: In an IPA study, the characteristics of your participants are very important, and for most studies you will be aiming for a homogenous sample of participants. What this means is that some people may volunteer to take part who you do not wish to interview. If there is a possibility that someone will not be interviewed after they have volunteered, this needs to be communicated as clearly as possible and as early as possible, for example, on advertising material, not just on information sheets.

Interpretation of data: In an IPA study you have to interpret your data, otherwise it isn't an IPA study. Most of the time you will be aiming to uncover the meaning your participants have of their experiences and you would hope that if/when they read your interpretations they would agree with them. However, some interpretations might go beyond something your participants might agree with. This might include interpretations of their unconscious processes, an observation of how your participants use language suggesting that their meanings of experiences might differ from the words they choose to describe those experiences, or in your development of themes that overlook something your participant considers crucial to the wider understanding. There are ways around this, such as participant checking, and staying close to the words used while using empathic interpretation, but in the end, IPA is an interpretative endeavour, and you must interpret your data. This is an ethical issue because it is rarely made clear to participants that this is what is going to be done with their data. We might mention analysis, we might even mention interpretation, but we rarely are explicit about what this means. There are examples in the literature, not necessarily IPA studies, where participants have ended up feeling very misunderstood, and even betrayed by the interpretation put on their words by researchers. The least we can do is aim to avoid this, and to make explicit to participants what we are going to do with their data.

Example: A focus on experience

Noonan, H, O'Donoghue, I, and Wilson, C. **Engaging with and navigating limbo: Lived experiences of siblings of adults with autism spectrum disorders.** *Journal of Applied Research in Intellectual Disabilities*, 2018 (31), 1144–1153. https://doi.org/10.1111/jar.12474

Hester knew what study she wanted to do from the start. She wanted to explore the lived experience of people who were siblings of autistic adults who also had intellectual disabilities. She also knew that she wanted to stay close to the lived experience phenomenologically, while being open to looking for meaning in the patterns across different participants' experience. There had been quite a lot of research including the voices of siblings of autistic children; some with child siblings and some with adult siblings, but there was less research including the voices of adult siblings of autistic adults. It was clear from the start that IPA was an appropriate method to use. The focus was on the lived experience of something that is important to the participants. Hester was interested in the idiographical approach of IPA and wanted to represent individual participants as well as looking for patterns across different participants.

The research decisions therefore were more practical than conceptual. Hester was in touch with someone who could support our recruitment through their service. This allowed us to contact potential participants without being concerned with trying to confirm diagnoses of their autistic sibling ourselves. As we wanted to foreground the experiences of the non-autistic sibling, this was important. Had we been in a position where we had to ensure that the autistic siblings had the relevant diagnosis, then we would have detracted from our focus. We aimed, and largely achieved, a homogenous sample of participants and developed an open-ended interview schedule.

The interviews were very moving, and Hester engaged in the analysis fully, holding the uncertainty as she developed possible themes and then worked further to develop these into the themes she reported. In IPA there is a double hermeneutic process between the researcher and the participant whereby the researcher is making sense of the participant's sense-making. One of the processes that can happen in research-team meetings or in supervision is a double hermeneutic between the primary researcher and the supervisor or research team. In this the research team is trying to make sense of the primary researcher's sense-making of the data. This can involve challenging themes, asking about their boundaries and properties. It can involve bringing in theories or other studies with which the results have resonance. It can involve reflecting on shared biases and on individual biases to help identify and bracket assumptions. It can also involve shared excitement, joy, anger, sadness and recognition as the results are discussed.

Further reading

Smith, J. A., Flowers, P., & Larkin, M. (2021) *Interpretative Phenomenological Analysis: Theory, method and research*, 2nd edition. London: SAGE.
Most things you need to know about IPA are in this book!

Smith, J. A. (2011) Evaluating the contribution of interpretative phenomenological analysis. *Health Psychology Review*, 5(1), 9–27. DOI: https://doi.org/10.1080/17437199.20 10.510659
Nizza, I. E., Farr, J., & Smith, J. A. (2021) Achieving excellence in interpretative phenomenological analysis (IPA): Four markers of high quality. *Qualitative Research in Psychology*, 18(3), 369–386.
These two papers highlight unique aspects of IPA and how to do it well!

15 Mixed methods research

If you have read several of the other chapters, then you might be reading this chapter because you can't decide on which method to choose and you are drawn to both the generalisability and empiricism of quantitative methods, while liking the richness, focus on context, and clinical relevance of qualitative methods. If you have come straight here, you might already be valuing both quantitative and qualitative methods in your work or reading. Mixed methods research isn't a new methodology, but there is a burgeoning literature on how to think about, develop, and analyse mixed methods research. It is essentially just mixing quantitative and qualitative research methods, but there are additional factors that you need to think about.

What is this approach?

At its simplest, mixed methods research involves mixing qualitative and quantitative methods. This could be within a single study, for example by using standardised measures, as well as interviewing participants. But it could also be within a set of studies, for example exploring relationships between variables in one study, and exploring the constructs themselves in interviews with participants in a different study. Technically any quantitative method can be combined with any qualitative method, but in reality, some pairings work better than others. This is explored further below and is described in Box 15.1.

Philosophy

You have to think hard about epistemology when you are planning and carrying out a mixed methods study. This is because it is within a mixed methods approach that you could be dealing with contrasting and perhaps even contradictory epistemologies. For example, for the quantitative part of your study you may be taking an empiricist or positivist stance, whereas in the qualitative part of your study you may be taking a constructionist stance. This is not necessarily a problem, but it needs to be thought about. Even at the planning stage of a mixed methods study, ask yourself which aspect of the study you are going to foreground and which results you will trust more. For example, if you are using mixed methods to evaluate your intervention, what results will you trust if your measures show very little change, but in your interviews your participants tell you how much they have learned and changed as a result of the interview? Most people lean one way or the other. Some of you will be thinking that if the measures don't show anything changed then the intervention doesn't work. Others will be thinking that if the participants report change, then the intervention does. Some of you might be natural mixed methods researchers and might be thinking, well maybe we used measures to capture the wrong things, maybe there is social desirability in the interview responses and participants have overstated the changes for the researcher's benefit. You will be searching for an understanding of the data that doesn't reject either of the findings, but instead integrates them into a richer understanding.

Critical realism is a philosophical position that is appropriate for mixed methods research as it explicitly states that knowledge is best when it comes from different perspectives and different directions. It is consistent with an approach that suggests that we get different but equally valuable information from different sources and through different kinds of analysis and that we come to a better understanding of something by integrating these different approaches.

If that isn't the way you are thinking about your data and your research, then different epistemological positions can be resolved. Pat Bazeley argues that all research is interpretative and the divide between quantitative and qualitative methods isn't as clear cut as we can present it to be. She argues that being open to different ways of thinking about data and research is crucial for mixed methods researchers. Therefore, interpreting your questionnaire data in one way and your interview data in another is fine, if you then work hard to integrate your understandings into a nuanced, contextual deeper understanding.

What kind of questions are best answered using this method?

The best kinds of questions to use mixed methods research to answer are complicated ones. They might be questions where you want to know both what and why of a phenomenon. It might be that you want a measure of the process, but also to understand the experience of it. You may want to think about mixed methods research if you have ever given out a survey (e.g., feedback on a service, gathering people's opinions on something) and included both forced-answer questions (e.g., how happy were you with the service on a scale of 1–10) with open-ended answers (e.g., tell us about your experience of the service). You may want to think about mixed methods research if you have interviewed people about their experiences, but also wanted to give them a score on a questionnaire to somehow quantify something about their experience. There are very few research questions that cannot be answered using mixed methods research. This doesn't mean that it is always the best approach, so it is worth understanding it better in order to make an informed choice (see Box 13.1 for some examples of how to decide which method is best for your question).

What are the key steps to using this method?

The first step in using mixed methods research is to **be very clear about your research question.** More than any other method, you must be very clear about what you want to find out. If you want to find out something about people's experiences as well as quantifying some aspect of this experience, then your research question may be best answered using mixed methods research. You may have some research hypotheses where you predict what you will find, but you may also have some more exploratory aspects to the question. That is perfect for a mixed methods study.

Even before you choose your quantitative and qualitative methods it is worth **reflecting on your research philosophy.** You need to be able to accept and integrate your findings from different sources of your research. If when you reflect on your own understanding of research you realise that you will always prioritise questionnaire or formal testing, or that you will always prioritise participants' reports of their own experiences, then mixed methods analysis might not be the best choice for you.

If you are still convinced that mixed methods research is for you, then the next step is to **decide what individual methods are best to combine.** Sometimes the research question makes this easy. Following the example started above – if you are evaluating your intervention, then you will need pre and post measures, possibly follow up measures, and you may or may not have a control group. You will likely either give out end of intervention surveys with open-ended questions, or if you have the resources you will talk to your participants about their experience of the group. Of course, there are ways of changing this, with interviews happening before and after the intervention, multiple baseline single case design approaches, or focus groups at end of intervention and at follow up, but the basic approach will be the same. For other research questions you will be choosing between an experimental approach or a model building/testing approach in combination with interviews or open-ended surveys. For analysis of your qualitative data, you may be choosing an approach that stays close to the data, or one that is deeply interpretative. All the steps involved in each of those methods will be taken, but there are some extra steps involved in mixed methods research.

After you have your methods chosen you need to make some decisions about **how you will collect, analyse and present your data.**

Will your *participants* for different aspects of the study be identical, overlapping, or non-overlapping? This is likely to be best answered by going back to the research question and working out whether the same participants can provide both quantitative and qualitative data to answer the question, whether you need all the participants who are providing quantitative data to provide qualitative data, or whether you need separate participants to answer different aspects of the same research question. Another aspect of this decision is to determine what you are asking of your participants and whether asking them to provide quantitative and qualitative data constitutes a significant burden, or whether they would have a preference.

Will you collect your data *sequentially or simultaneously*? This is not about whether you will collect one type of data first from an individual participant, but about the wider timing of your data collection. Will you collect all your quantitative data first, analyse it and then use your qualitative data to explore the results further (or vice versa), or will you collect your data at the same time and analyse it together?

Weighting of the data. In your integration of your results will your data be equally weighted, or will you be foregrounding or prioritising one type of data?

After you have decided on your individual methods, how you will sequence them and how you will involve your participants, *then* you will get your **ethical approval, recruit your participants, and carry out your data collection**. These are all considered more fully in the chapters on individual approaches and I recommend you read the chapters relevant to your methods as well as this one.

When you have your data and have performed preliminary analyses using your chosen approach, then you need to work out how to **integrate your results and how to present them**. O'Cathain and colleagues (see further reading) suggest different ways of doing this such as following a thread or using a mixed methods matrix, but there are others and you should be driven by your research question. Mixed methods research can be a political choice (especially if using transformative approaches as described below), and therefore the presentation of the research is a fundamental part of the process.

How does this method usually go wrong and what can you do about it?

As well as the burden on participants (discussed above), the main issue with mixed methods research is the burden on the researcher to be good at both types of research. You will need statistical analysis skills, qualitative analysis skills, a capacity for managing uncertainty and holding multiple possibilities in mind as well as all the other research skills needed for applied studies. You need good project and data management skills, and you also need to be able to write in a concise, convincing way. The main way of dealing with this difficulty is to ensure you are as prepared as possible to undertake mixed methods research. Part of this is knowing what your own strengths are in terms of research and either having experience in both types of analysis or being willing to learn. Overcoming these difficulties can also be about choosing the right people to work with – so different aspects of the study can be developed by different members of the research team. As a student, it might involve choosing a suitable supervisory team.

Box 15.1: Types of mixed methods research designs

Sequential
One part of the study comes before the other

Quantitative to qualitative – this is an **explanatory** design

Qualitative to quantitative – this is an **exploratory** design

Concurrent
Both the quantitative data and qualitative data are collected at the same time

If both are equally important and analysis integrates both – this is a **triangulation** design

If one is more important than the other, and the second is just to enhance the understanding – this is an **embedded** design

In addition, you can use any of these designs within a **transformative** framework. By applying vision, advocacy, ideology and a framework any mixed methods approach can be used to transform understanding.

The other thing that very commonly goes wrong in mixed methods research is that one aspect of the research is much less well developed than the other. This could be in sample size, where quantitative data is collected, but the sample size is just too small for statistical analysis. It could be that the quantitative data is excellent, but the qualitative data is not rich enough for proper analysis or the analysis is only done at a surface-level. In mixed methods research you need to minimise weaknesses with your participant recruitment, your choice of measures, your analysis of the data and your integration and interpretation of the results.

Finally, if you haven't reflected on your own positioning, your final write up may give you away. Using deterministic language when the study is cross-sectional or making conclusions based on only one kind of data are common errors in mixed methods studies. The more you can reflect on your own assumptions, the less these will be problems in your study.

What are the practical issues associated with this method?

The practical issues associated with this method depend on the design you choose. If you are simply collecting questionnaire and open-ended survey questions from all your participants, there are no additional practical issues. However, if you want to recruit two separate groups of participants then the success of your study is dependent on two different recruitment drives. If you need your participants to complete measures and take part in interviews at two different times, then you need to work hard at developing your relationships with your participants in order to keep them interested in the research long enough to complete both aspects of the research.

For good mixed methods research you also need a good mix of skills in the research team. Unless you have a mixed methods researcher on the team, you will need experts in both quantitative and qualitative analysis on the team. The more people on the team, the more difficult it can be to coordinate meetings or deadlines. Also, if you are working with quantitative and qualitative research experts it might be your job to do the work to integrate the results. As well as complications coordinating meetings and deadlines, it might be your job to work with your team to determine a joint epistemology and ontology and to negotiate how the results are interpreted and written up.

Ethics

The ethical issues inherent in mixed methods research are those discussed above in other chapters, with the additional complication of having multiple methods and/or multiple participant groups.

Example: Neither experiment nor interviews enough by themselves

Rickard, E, Hevey, D, Wilson, C. (2021). **The impact of seating arrangement and therapy task on therapeutic alliance formation.** *Counselling and Psychotherapy Research*, **21**, **683–696.** https://doi.org/10.1002/capr.12341

In one of his placements within his clinical psychology training, Eoin found himself learning a new approach for working with people who were suicidal, the Collaborative Assessment and Management of Suicidality (CAMS). One of the things that struck him was that unlike a lot of experiences of doing psychotherapy, in the CAMS model there are times where you sit side by side with your client, rather than facing them. Eoin's own experience of this was important. It felt different to the usual way of working, mostly in a good way, but there were some things that also didn't feel as comfortable. He went to the literature to make sense of it, but there was very little about seating arrangement that took an empirical approach. There were lots of people writing about it from a clinical or therapeutic perspective, but little empirical research.

It was mainly the lack of empirical studies in this topic that drew Eoin to explore the idea of an experimental study. It seemed like something that it was possible to easily manipulate without having to deceive participants about the aim of the study. It was possible to manipulate the variable without putting anyone at risk as neither option – sitting side by side or sitting opposite each other – was known to be better or worse than the other. Once we knew we could manipulate seating position within an experiment we needed to determine what our outcome measure was and whether we needed to be completely open about it, or whether we could embed it in other aspects of the experiment. Eoin had noticed that within his clinical work using the CAMS model, the side-by-side work was often completing paperwork, whereas it was common to move back to a face-to-face position for talking. He wanted to incorporate this into the design as it was such an important confounding variable. Thus, the experiment started to take shape; we had two conditions, face-to-face versus side-by-side seating arrangement, and completing questionnaires or answering questions. We could randomise people into four groups based on these conditions and get the answers we need for our outcome as part of the procedure – using the questionnaires or interview questions. As there were likely to be learning effects on any measures it didn't seem appropriate to use our participants in two of the conditions, so we randomised the participant sample into the four different groups. Thus, the experiment came together.

However, although this was an important study in its own right, Eoin had two concerns. One was that it would involve an analogue sample and not those who had experienced therapy, and the second was that it only manipulated two of the variables that might be contributing to the experience for participants. I had typically introduced a qualitative component into an experimental design within a debriefing process, but that would not solve either of these problems. Thus, Eoin decided that it would be worth doing a mixed methods study and to add a qualitative interview component to his overall study. With a separate, but overlapping set of participants Eoin completed qualitative interviews about seating positions in therapy and participants were invited to talk more broadly about the conditions that are conducive to good therapeutic sessions.

Eoin had to battle with all the difficulties of doing a mixed methods study. He needed two separate participant groups with different characteristics. For the experiment he needed the physical situation to be as identical as possible, but for the qualitative interviews it was more relaxed. He needed to understand the methodologies and analysis strategies for both, with skills in statistics, experimental design as well as qualitative analysis. And finally, he needed skills in combining results in a mixed methods study. However, in the results the two studies complemented each other, and it was only by putting both parts of the study together that a greater understanding was reached.

Further reading

Books

Creswell, J. W. (2014) *A Concise Introduction to Mixed Methods Research*. Thousand Oaks, CA: Sage.

Tashakkori, A. & Teddlie, C. (2010) *SAGE Handbook of Mixed Methods in Social & Behavioral Research*. Thousand Oaks, CA: Sage.

Bazeley, P. (2017) *Integrating Analyses in Mixed Methods Research*. London: Sage.

Papers

O'Cathain, A., Murphy, E., & Nicholl, J. (2010). Three techniques for integrating data in mixed methods studies. *BMJ*, 341.

Hanson, W. E., Creswell, J. W., Clark, V. L. P., Petska, K. S., & Creswell, J. D. (2005). Mixed methods research designs in counseling psychology. *Journal of Counseling Psychology*, 52(2), 224–235. DOI: https://doi.org/10.1037/0022-0167.52.2.224

Johnson, R. B., & Onwuegbuzie, A. J. (2004). Mixed methods research: A research paradigm whose time has come. *Educational Researcher*, 33(7), 14–26. DOI: https://doi.org/10.3102/0013189X033007014

Also check out https://mmira.wildapricot.org/ for the international association for mixed methods research.

16 Dissemination of your work

There are lots of reasons to disseminate your research. Communicating what you have found with others is likely to be part of your intention in doing research. However, there are also ethical reasons for disseminating your research. Your participants have given their time, energy and expertise to help you understand something better. They may also have contributed to you getting a qualification, and they may have been involved in other aspects of the research. Other people may also have contributed to your research, perhaps intellectually by helping design the study or helping with the analysis, or perhaps practically by helping you access participants or resources. Given that, there is some ethical imperative to disseminate the results of your study to justify their time and effort.

Applied psychological research rarely happens in a vacuum. There are stakeholders involved in the planning stages of the research or in the recruitment of participants, and even beyond the stakeholders there are other professionals who are likely to benefit from understanding what you have found. Most research is written up somewhere, but how we write up our research, in what format, using what language depends on our audience. We might want to communicate with our participants, other stakeholders, professionals more broadly, our own professional discipline, all professionals working with our participant groups, or to the world itself. All these audiences have different needs and respond to different kinds of information. Therefore, when planning your dissemination strategy, you need to start by thinking of your audience and what you need them to know. If you start with what you know, you are likely to fall into the traps of being too formal and technical for some and being too informal and not providing sufficient details for others. In this chapter, three different strategies are outlined. They are not exhaustive, and they may not be suitable for your own audience, but the principles in each section may help you think about dissemination from your audience's point of view.

Communicating with stakeholders

Chances are, along the way, your research involved other stakeholders beyond yourself. For some people this might just be an institutional supervisor, but for others it will be a whole team of interested professionals, or a team of people with lived experience, or a combination of the two. In many applied settings these people do not come from a single professional background and do not have the same research training that you do. Furthermore, it might be that you want to communicate your research to other audiences that it impacts directly such as professionals in different services that work with similar populations. Some of these people do not want to read your college dissertation or thesis. They do not want to read a formal academic paper. What they want is an accessible account of what you did and what you found.

What does your audience need to know?

What your audience needs to know depends on who they are. If you are talking to or writing for a group of professional psychologists, you can assume a certain knowledge of psychological theory and of standard research procedures and methods. You can also assume that they use similar shorthands and metaphors. If the people you are communicating with are like you, whether that is professionally, or in terms of their experiences (if you are an insider researcher), it might be quite easy to work out what you think they need to know.

If you are talking to, or writing for, your participants or the public, they will not necessarily have this knowledge. Furthermore, there will likely be a wider variety of knowledge and experience in the group. People in this group are likely to want to know more about what contribution they made, and what you found. You might want to take more time talking about who took part and the practicalities of what the participants did to take part in the research, rather than the psychometric properties of your measures and your sophisticated statistical techniques! You are likely to spend most of your time talking about what you found and what this means. Your participants are also likely to want to know what else you are going to do with the results of your research. Few of us ever do research that makes a huge difference, but sometimes the small things can be impactful, but only if we disseminate to the relevant people.

Finally, if you are talking to or writing for mixed professional groups there might be areas of specific expertise that they have that you don't, as well as areas of expertise that you have gained, having completed the research. These groups may be the most difficult to plan for in terms of what they need to know about your research because their own professional background, their own research training and their motivation for taking time to learn about your research will vary most. However, this can be freeing; if it isn't clear what your audience needs to know, then you have more freedom to tell them what you find interesting. If they are professionals working with your participant group, then this is your chance to help them understand the topic of your research and think about how it applies to their own practice. You might have to describe the psychological theory underpinning your research more fully, you might have to describe your participants carefully so the audience feels that your research is credible, and you might have to describe not just what you found, but what it means.

Ways of communicating the message

There are lots of different ways of communicating with different audiences. We often get trapped into thinking about research reports, either as pieces of written work for our qualifications, or as journal articles for publication in largely inaccessible journals. However, communicating with a wider audience than our academic assessors or an international academic audience means we can think creatively about dissemination modalities.

Brief reports and newsletters

A brief report or newsletter may be a very accessible way of communicating with your audience. It can get straight to the point, include colour, pictures, photos, or quotes, and be a bit more creative than a formal report. It doesn't require much of your audience in terms of their time or attention but gets your message across very quickly and hopefully clearly. The difficult aspect of writing a newsletter or brief report is deciding what to put in and what to leave out. A brief report might be 500 or so words, maybe 1000, but that is likely to be 10–20 per cent of a full report so you really need to think about what goes in and what doesn't go in. Thinking about what your audience needs to know is crucial in this. It often doesn't work that well to present a brief report that is just a very sparsely written summary of your research. This can come across as cold and divorced from the important message. If you are worried that people haven't got the full details of the research then try pairing a brief report or newsletter with access to a longer report, either by having the longer report online where it can be accessed by anyone, or by sending it on by request.

Talks

When planning a talk, try to talk directly to your audience rather than just telling them generic things about your research. This ensures that your audience hears the message. If you send out a newsletter or brief report, there is no guarantee that anyone will read it. If you talk to an audience, all of them (or nearly) will listen to what you have to say. In addition, in a talk the audience get to ask questions and you get to clarify anything that isn't clear. The downside of a talk is that it is usually transient – once you have finished the talk the audience don't have any record they can go back to, to remember what you said. You can supplement your talk with a report to leave with the audience. Professional audiences might want links to published papers, or they might just want a copy of your slides.

When you are giving a talk about your research then you can draw on your own creativity in your slide design, in the structure of your talk, and in your presentation style. Sometimes we resort to slides full of words because we think that is what we have to present, or because it feels safer, but it might not be the best way of communicating with your audience. The other trap we often fall into is cramming a lot of information into talks to try and make sure everyone has all the information they need, but then running out of time for questions or losing some of the enthusiasm for the work in the detail. You cannot get all the information about the study into a 10-minute, 30-minute or even 1-hour talk, so instead of trying to do this, try to work out what your audience needs to know.

Longer reports

Sometimes a longer report is the best way of communicating with our audience. This does not mean it has to be written as a dissertation or a journal article. We can still foreground the needs of the audience in a longer report, it is just a chance to put more detail in. Some of the features that might distinguish a longer report for stakeholders from an academic article are the language used, the structure of the report, and the use of pictures, figures and other illustrations.

Communicating with an academic audience

If you are doing your research as part of a qualification it is likely that you are embedded in an academic institution. That means that there is likely good support for the usual academic ways of disseminating your research: journal articles and conference presentations. There may also be more local ways of disseminating your research such as journal clubs, internal presentations; however, how to present to these audiences is likely to be the same as other academic audiences. If you are primarily a practitioner, then there is likely less support for academic publishing within your institution, and it might be that you can draw on a wider research team to support this aspect of dissemination.

Writing journal articles

Writing for academic dissemination holds a different intention compared to writing for stakeholders. When you are writing for stakeholders you want to communicate about your findings and how you got them. When you are writing for an academic audience you are trying to further scientific understanding of the topic. To do this, you need to create a strong argument for the study, describe your method clearly, present your results well, and draw valid conclusions from them. Which of these is most important does depend on the research method you have chosen. If you have compared two groups of people in your research, then you will need a strong argument and close attention to describing your participants. If you have done an experiment you will have to describe your method, including your procedure very carefully, and if you have done an interpretative qualitative study you will have to write about your themes convincingly and include writing on your own positionality.

Unlike communicating with stakeholders, communicating with an academic audience requires more attention to your method and results including paying attention to reliability, validity, trustworthiness, transparency of method and analysis, and generalisability. Journal articles often want you to reflect on the strengths and limitations of your study, which demonstrates further awareness of your own method and what it does and doesn't do.

Writing up research for an academic audience also requires transparency. If you are writing up quantitative research you need to provide sufficient information in order that the study could be replicated. This kind of transparency fits with quality markers of quantitative research. If you are writing up qualitative research, transparency involves a wider range of features including a reflexivity section, a full description of the process of collecting the data and of analysing the data and providing evidence for your analysis in the form of themes. Unlike in quantitative research where it can be helpful to provide official details, like psychometric properties of your measures, in qualitative research it is more transparent to describe your analysis fully, rather than summarise the steps that the text-book describes.

Sometimes you may have more content than is allowed by the word count, but that is important for readers to have access to. This can be where supplementary files can be helpful. Many journals allow supplementary files to be submitted alongside the article and these can be accessed from the journal's online portal. These may include more extensive tables, for example when undertaking sub-group analyses in a meta-analysis, or a CONSORT flow diagram in an intervention study, or perhaps more information about the participants or baseline data. A journal's guide for authors will let you know what they expect you to submit and also what you are allowed to submit as supplementary files.

Writing journal articles requires you to use a certain kind of academic language and this can be tricky for some people, especially if they have taken non-standard routes through higher and further education, or if it is a long while since they were in education. However, the advantage here is that by doing research you are likely to be reading a lot of research and you certainly have access to lots of papers. This can help you shape your own expectations of what language to use for a journal article.

Finally, writing articles and getting them published, especially when the research is applied research, can be a long and thankless exercise. You may need to submit the same paper to several journals before you find one that will publish it. You will need to respond to reviewers, some of whom are excellent and have helpful comments that improve your work, but some of whom will not understand why you are doing the research and will be critical without being helpful. Even the early stages of submitting a paper to a journal can be difficult. You need to log into the journal portal, setting yourself up on their system. You often need to have separate cover pages, anonymised versions of the manuscript, as well as key words, a separate abstract, and sometimes suggestions for reviewers. When you have submitted several papers, this becomes easier, but at first it takes a long time, and there is little forewarning that submission involves all these stages. The *information for authors* that all journals have can indicate some of these prior to submission – it will certainly detail what you need to have in your submission – but some of them are unexpected. If you are doing this for the first time it is certainly worth putting aside a full morning or afternoon for it.

Choosing a journal

There are lots of journals out there and it can be hard to navigate the choice you have. You can start to develop a list of options by checking out where the papers you cite in your paper have been published, or you can simply search online for journals in your topic or using your methodology. There are a few places that keep relevant lists of journals, and these can also be found through internet searches.

Once you have a list of potential journals there are several things to consider when choosing one to submit your research to.

Impact factors. An impact factor is an imperfect measure of the quality of a journal. It is a metric that measures how often each paper in the journal is cited by other papers. A journal that consistently publishes papers that are well cited is likely to claim a high status. However, a lot of factors determine how much a paper is cited, and therefore the impact factor of certain journals. If your career does depend on publishing, work out whether you (or your supervisor) need(s) to aim for a journal with a certain impact factor and take that into account when you choose your journal. Most people doing applied psychological research are not driven by impact factors, but usually the larger the impact factor, the harder it is to get your paper accepted, so even if you do not need to aim for a particular impact factor, they can be helpful in choosing which journal is right for you.

Predatory journals. Predatory journals are those that solicit papers from authors and charge them for publishing their paper. Lots of non-predatory journals charge authors for publishing their papers open-access – that means anyone can read and download the article, not just someone who purchases the journal or has access to it via their institution, and there are obvious advantages of publishing open-access. This allows researchers who do not have access to journals to access your paper, and it also means more people are likely to read it. However, the difference between a non-predatory journal and a predatory journal is in the soliciting of papers directly, and the reviewing process. However difficult the reviewing process is for an author, it does add a layer of accountability and checking of research. In predatory journals there is very little genuine reviewing, and all papers are accepted. You are likely to find your paper in among unrelated papers, making it harder to find by other researchers and practitioners, and you will find yourself out of pocket for that privilege! Avoid these journals. If it isn't clear whether something is predatory or not, try searching online to see. You can often find blogs and website that have lists of journals to avoid and why.

Topic versus methodology. One of the main issues I deal with in publishing applied psychological research is whether to focus on the topic or whether to focus on the methodology when choosing a journal. For example, as well as

journals dedicated to every psychological topic under the sun, there are journals dedicated to publishing qualitative research, or mixed methods research,
or experimental research. Your topic will often span several topics, for example, much of my research is developmental and clinical, so you have to choose
which one to focus on. To decide, I would focus on who you want your audience
to be. Have you a message for practitioners or for other researchers in a topic,
or have you found something that would be interesting to other people using
your method? For example, if I have done a qualitative study on parents of
children with cystic fibrosis, do I want to communicate with people who read
qualitative studies, or those who work with children with cystic fibrosis, or
those who work with parents? You may not have this kind of choice, but if you
do, think about who your audience is.

Checking the journal for hints as to what is accepted. Some journals have
preferences for certain types of studies, such as quantitative studies or experimental studies. Others exclude review papers or single case design. Sometimes
this is made explicit in the title of the journal or the aims of the journal, but
sometimes it is more implicit. Sometimes it can be found in the wording in
instructions for authors or the guide for authors. Wording such as 'driven by
strong hypotheses' means that the journal is unlikely to publish qualitative
research. Sometimes it can be found in what is not in the list of articles they
do publish, for example, in one journal there might be instructions for review
papers, case studies and research articles, but in another there is no reference
to case studies.

The other way of checking to see what a journal is happy to publish is to
check what they have recently published. Have a look through their list of
recently published articles and see if they have published one like yours. 'Like
yours' might mean using your methodology or it might mean with the same
kind of participants as the ones in your study. You might want to check out
whether all the published articles have very large sample sizes, or whether
they all use complex statistical techniques. Checking out what the journal has
published over the past few years gives you a very good idea of what kinds of
research they accept for publication.

The final thing to check is how many words or pages you are given to write
up your research and whether this does or doesn't include tables, figures, and
references. If the word count is small, then it is unlikely that they are expecting
in-depth qualitative research studies to be submitted. If there is a strict limit
on tables, then they are not expecting detailed quantitative research. This is a
factor also worth thinking about in your own writing. Some journals do have
a limited word count but are happy to publish qualitative studies. If this is the
case, are you happy writing something with such a limited word count? What
might you have to miss out in writing it this way?

Responding to reviewers

Responding to reviewers is an art in itself. Some journals are now providing
good advice on how to do this, for example, by tabulating each comment from

each reviewer and indicating how you have responded to it. You do not need to do everything that a reviewer suggests, but you do need to think about everything they say and think about whether you need to change anything, how to change it, and if you do not need to change it, by providing a rationale for this in your response to the editor. I have seen responses to reviewers that are longer than the paper itself! Most people who write papers regularly get used to the process, even if it still hurts when someone is very critical, but if you haven't had many papers published or this is your first submission, then getting reviewer comments back can be where everything stalls. This is where your research team can be helpful. You may be able to divvy up the different editing jobs and share out the work, but mostly, the research team will likely share your frustrations and you can let off steam within the team prior to responding carefully and thoughtfully to your reviewers. It is worth remembering that although editors do their very best to send your manuscript to experts, you are still the person who did the study, and you have expertise too. If your paper is rejected because of negative reviewer comments give yourself time to absorb them, take notice of the ones that you think improve your work, make any changes that you think will improve the manuscript and try a different journal.

Presenting at conferences

There are usually two ways to present at conferences: an oral presentation or talk, and a poster. Sometimes the oral presentation is part of a symposium, which is a few papers with a theme presented together. These are usually organised and submitted by one or two people who ask others to join them because they share an interest in the same topic. You might have a personal preference for one or the other, but the key differences I would consider are that getting a space to present a poster is usually easier, but you often get a wider audience for a talk.

Giving an academic talk (single paper or within a symposium)

Giving a talk in a conference involves a combination of considering what your audience needs to know, as described above, with giving enough detail about your method and analysis to allow people to evaluate the validity of your findings. There are conferences that cover a very wide variety of topics within psychology, often organised by a professional body. People attending these conferences could come from any discipline in psychology and so you need to think about what specialist knowledge you have about your discipline that you will need to explain to allow it to be accessible to all your audience. There are population specific conferences where lots of different professions attend to learn the latest research all about their population. For this you need to think about what psychology offers to the understanding of your population. Finally, there are some conferences that are small and specific; these might be called research days or research meetings. These are the conferences where you are most likely to have an audience that understands your research and so you can really showcase your own knowledge and expertise without worrying too much about the audience.

If you can, being part of a symposium can be a lovely introduction to talking at a conference. Being among other people who are interested in the same topic as you are, can feel very containing. At least you will have an audience and at least they will be interested to hear what you have to say! Symposiums tend to be organised by more senior people, but this is only because they are somewhat more likely to have the connections to invite people to be part of them. If you know other researchers in your topic, then there is no problem with organising the symposium yourself.

Presenting a poster at an academic conference

An academic poster is simply a visual way of presenting your research. They are usually printed in large format, such as A1 or A0, so that you can include a lot of the detail if you want to. Indeed, some posters appear to be a short paper written very small, so it fits on a large sheet on paper. However, a poster is an opportunity for you to communicate your research in creative ways. Most people don't want lots of detail in a poster – they will look for a published paper for that – what you want a poster to do is to attract someone to come and look at it, and to provide sufficient detail for them to be interested and talk to you further. A few years ago, Mike Morrison proposed a new way of visually presenting academic posters that foregrounded the findings from a research study and had other features that support dissemination such as use of QR codes to link to a full report. These have become popular with some researchers. If this way of presenting your poster doesn't appeal, then at least it has opened the possibility of being creative in your poster presentations, and for not trying to include every possible detail.

The aim of your poster is to both attract people to it to talk to you and to learn more, and to impart knowledge to the people attending the conference. These two aims can conflict; pictures, good use of colour, catchy titles, and clear findings foregrounded are good at attracting people to the poster, and a clear description of the research including what you did, why, and what you found, are good at imparting knowledge. The best posters do both.

How do you choose which conference(s) to go to?

Choosing conferences to go to depends on finances, your availability to travel (if the conference is not virtual), and who you want to hear about your research. Sometimes your institution will have funding available for students to present at conferences, but often you have to think ahead as you may only be ready to present your research at the end of your course (unless you are doing a PhD or extended research project) and you may not be able to apply for the funding after you have completed the course. When you are thinking about funding the conference you need to think about the conference registration fee, the travel (if there is any), accommodation and subsistence and anything else you need to be able to travel or present. You are unlikely to need a laptop or something to present on, but there may be additional expenses for you, for example if you need to travel with disability aids you may need checked baggage and you may need taxis from affordable accommodation to the conference centre. You may want to attend a conference dinner or party. You may need visas to travel to certain countries depending on your own country of origin. Most conferences haven't even started to think about childcare, and so there may also be expenses to leave people behind to have them minded or otherwise cared for. The rise in virtual conferences that was necessary during COVID-19 has made them more accessible for many, either financially or personally, but many organisations are now going back to face-to-face conferences.

If you do have choices of conferences given these considerations, then you get to choose who you want to talk to. Are you wanting an expert audience who can really help you think about the research, its strengths and weaknesses and where to take it next? Do you want to present to people who work with your participant population to try and influence them to do something different? Or do you want to let other psychologists know about a new population or something new about that population to increase their awareness and knowledge? Just as choosing a journal involves thinking about who you want to share your knowledge with, so does choosing a conference.

Communicating using social media

Even disseminating our research using the above strategies only gets our message out to a very small number of people. It is perhaps for that reason that more and more people are using social media to advertise their research more widely. There is a cynical view of this, that it is self-promotion and serves the needs of the person advertising the research. An even more cynical view is that it is supported by, or even required by, certain institutions for their purposes. However, even if these are true, advertising your research more widely does have other purposes. Professionals who do not have access to library journals, or who cannot attend conferences, can use social media to find out about research happening in their line of work. Participants and participant advocacy groups often do not have access to much research at all, and so dissemination through social media can empower populations with knowledge that is largely inaccessible through traditional academic routes. Finally, by sharing your ideas you can support other psychologists to think more broadly about doing research, about research methods for different kinds of knowledge, and about different topics in psychology. Sometimes this cross-fertilisation of ideas can lead to the most fruitful research programmes!

Methods of dissemination across social media

This section is most likely to go out of date quickest, but the key issues about writing for your audience stay the same!

X (was Twitter)[1]

X (formerly known as Twitter) encourages you to think in short bursts. Each tweet can be a maximum of 280 characters, which was increased from 140 characters in 2017. However, far from making people report their research in a couple of sentences, this seems to have encouraged people to write up their research as twitter threads. This is a series of tweets describing the research. The format is therefore short and concise, but the content can vary from technical – mainly trying to communicate with similar scientists – to lay accounts – mainly trying to communicate with people with no background in your discipline. The other way in which X is commonly used is to advertise a published report. This could be an academic paper, a pre-print of a paper, or publication of a report that is publicly available. Sometimes the key results of the paper are put into tweets, but with a link to the full report. Some research has suggested that this kind of dissemination leads to increased downloads, increased reads and increased citations. Unless this is important in your own professional life, then that perhaps doesn't matter as much as getting the results out to a wide audience and making them available to your participant group across the world.

The great thing about X is that it is easily available. Creating tweets is relatively easy – if you have written a report about your research, you can write the tweets! And the coverage is huge with approximately 400 million users at time of writing. The disadvantage is that X appears to encourage polarisation of views and pile-ons. If there is anything controversial or uncomfortable about your research, you might find yourself receiving a lot of attention that is negative and unconstructive and can even be downright offensive or abusive.

YouTube

There are some fantastic videos uploaded to YouTube explaining research. Indeed, TED talks are often based on someone's body of research to date. There are videos of conference talks, and in recent times lots of videos of university lectures that are grounded in research. If you get to talk about your research then recording it, if the occasion allows it, and uploading it, gives you something to refer people to if they want to know more. All these ways of using YouTube capitalise on recordings that are happening for some other reason, but there are ways of creating content on YouTube that are specific to dissemination. These could use animation, or they could have lots of different sections edited together. These videos take a lot longer to create – Mike Morrison who has created a YouTube video about his new way of presenting academic posters says it took him a year to create it! - but they can get a lot of views. They are also fun to create and fun to watch. If the aim is to get the message out there, this kind of video might be better at doing that compared to someone watching you stand up and talk about your research.

---

1 At the time of writing X (Twitter) still exists, although there has been some movement of academics to Mastadon.

LinkedIn, ResearchGate and other work-based platforms

Your important networks might not be social media networks. LinkedIn, ResearchGate and other work-based platforms may be your usual outlet for giving and receiving information on your work-interests. The advantage of these platforms is that you have built the networks yourself and therefore you have a good understanding of your audience. Furthermore, because they *are* work-related networks, they are likely to be receptive to your message. Many practitioners are part of these networks but would not use social media or read academic journals.

If you are writing for these work-related networks, then you need to adapt your language and writing style for them. This should be one of the easiest platforms to write for as it will be consistent with your professional work and/or studies. It is worth noting that most people on these platforms skim read posts or read the first couple of paragraphs of a post, so it might be worth keeping it brief, but you will know your audience and how to write for them.

Blogs, Vlogs, Podcasts, Webinars

If you are creative and adventurous, then you may want to create your own content. This could include blogs, which tend to be written words, vlogs, which are visual recordings, podcasts which are auditory or voice recordings, and webinars which involve visual recordings, but are most likely to include more formal aspects of academic presentation.

These have blossomed in the past few years as the technology to create these has become widely available and people have sought different ways of improving their knowledge. Sometimes these approaches can be hosted on an institutional website or a personal website. At other times you may need to use available software or platforms, such as WordPress, WIX or Square Space.

The advantage of these is that the format is up to you. They can be short or long, full of information or having a single simple message, visually and auditorily appealing or simple and unfussy. This can also be a disadvantage; if you aren't used to combining your creative talents with your work skills this might seem daunting!

Final comments on dissemination

You have done some great research and other people deserve to know about that! Think about who your audiences are and write for them. Think about your message and make sure that you prioritise that. Think about who your participants were and ensure that they have access to your findings. Play to your strengths and be creative. You never know, in the conversations you have with others about your research you might find your next research idea!

Further reading

https://astrobites.org/2020/02/28/fixing-academic-posters-the-betterposter-approach/
Read all about how to make a better poster

http://www.professionalpalliativehub.com/research/palliative-care-research-projects/
developing-implementing-%E2%80%98system%E2%80%99-structured-network-wide
A structured approach to dissemination. The focus is on palliative care, but the principles are wide-ranging

https://guides.library.vcu.edu/c.php?g=480243&p=6785181
A great practical dissemination planning guide

Epilogue: The end or just another beginning?

Congratulations! You have got to the end of the book. I hope that also means you have got to the end of your research project. My aim with this book was to help you work through the different things you need to think about in planning, carrying out, and disseminating your research, and here you are at the end so why do we need an epilogue? Well, in doing your research you will have learned lots of things that will help you with your next research project, but also, in doing your research you have probably ended up with more questions than you started with! This final section aims to bring together the themes of the book to help you think about your next research project and to help you learn from the research project you have just done.

Alignment in research

A key theme in the book is **alignment**. A good research project aligns the original observation with the research question, which in turn aligns with the method chosen, and the analysis performed. If you think about your recent research project, ask yourself how well your chosen method answered your research question and whether your results of your analysis helped you understand your topic. Before you undertake your next research project have a think about whether, if you started again, you would ask the same research question. Think about which other approaches you could have chosen to answer the question, and which one you would choose now. If you would choose a different approach, then as well as asking whether it would answer your research question better, it is worth asking why. The answer to why might be about the practicalities of doing the research.

The next section might help you answer that.

Play to your strengths

Research often takes a lot of time. It also takes commitment, both in terms of intellectual engagement, but also emotional engagement. Therefore, it is worth playing to your strengths. Throughout the book, the sections on what might go wrong highlight the importance of planning ahead, of giving yourself time to complete analyses, of working with your supervisor or team (see below for more on this), and knowing enough about the method you choose to be confident in using it. When you reflect on the research you have done you might be able to identify what went wrong quite easily, but it might be harder to identify what you did well. You can learn from both of these reflections. When you identify what didn't go well or was difficult you might find that there are lots of reasons to explain this. It could have been that you just needed more time or more planning. It could have been that you didn't get the buy in from the research team in the way you needed. It could have been that you got lost in the method and ended up feeling confused and worried. At this stage it should be clear which of those problems are easily fixed, and which you could choose to avoid next time. If you didn't get buy in from the research team, can you do something that doesn't require the same amount of buy in? If you ran out of time to do an in-depth analysis, could you choose to do quantitative research or a less inductive qualitative approach? In my experience most people finish a research project with a list of things they are never going to do again in a research project. It is worth thinking about what you *do* want to do again as well.

At the end of the research process it is also worth going back to the beginning in terms of your passion for the subject. Sometimes in the messiness and practicality of doing research we forget why we are doing it and what we are passionate about. Caring about something enough to do research about is a strength, so play to it.

Look after your participants

Getting the right number of the right kind of participant is often the most stressful part of a research project. Whether it is collecting large numbers of participants for cross-sectional research, or a homogenous sample for IPA, recruiting participants is often the hardest aspect of research. However, working with participants is often the most rewarding aspect of research. If you are doing applied psychological research it is likely you will be working with people, and therefore doing research with people feels meaningful. In reflecting on your previous research project certain participants, or certain tasks you got people to do might stand out in your memory. These can give you insights into how well you looked after your participants. What did you ask them to do? Was this reasonable and were you clear with them about it? Did they know what to expect at the beginning and understand what their involvement had been at the end when you debriefed them? Were you ever left wanting to check in with someone a week later to check they were OK because of what they shared with you? And did you check in? Would any of them be interested in consulting on a new research project in the topic? As well as learning about your own strengths in research, reflecting on your participants' experience of taking part in your research project can help you make it better next time.

Care about diversity and inclusion

If you look at your whole sample of participants, were you happy with the variety of people who took part? In experimental studies and IPA studies you are likely to want a homogenous sample of participants. In Grounded Theory you want a heterogenous sample. In other studies you are likely to want a representative sample. Representative in applied psychological research means representative not only of the demographic characteristics of the sample from which yours is drawn, but also representative with respect to the topic, for example, with respect to disease/syndrome, personal characteristics, or experiential characteristics. In order to determine this you need to ask questions of your sample that reflect these characteristics. When you reflect on your participant sample can you identify who you didn't reach/recruit who you would have liked to? And can you identify what you wished you had asked them about themselves in order to determine how representative they were of the population they are drawn from?

As well as thinking about diversity and inclusion in our participant sample it is worth thinking a little about diversity and inclusion in researchers. We are a privileged group and hold power simply by being the person doing the research. We don't often think about who gets to create new knowledge and who that knowledge is created for. I am not an expert, but I can highly recommend the three books in the Further reading section as a starting point if you are interested in thinking about this topic.

Use your team/supervisor/colleagues

There is a beautiful myth of the lone genius discovering unique things about the world, ploughing their lonely but intellectual furrow and being brilliant. In reality, most research happens because a group of people come together to talk, think, plan and carry out research. Not only does this make it a less lonely pursuit, it also makes the research less subject to individual biases (but perhaps more subject to group biases!), less likely to have major flaws, and also be more creative and inclusive. Developing a team of people who want to work with you on a project, who care about the same things you do, and who will support *and* challenge you is very valuable in doing research. Different people have different roles in a research team and if everyone works to their own strengths, but with the same end-goal, the result will be a better research project. In a good research team you want someone who pays attention to detail, someone who is happy playing devil's advocate, someone who is willing to do the everyday work, someone who has a good overview and of course someone who holds the hope, the positivity and the energy, especially when things are tricky! These don't have to be different people; one person can play lots of roles in a research team. If you think back over your last research project can you identify, either from this list or just from your own thoughts, who you were missing in your team? Who did you really value and what role(s) did they play? What were your own roles within the team and which were you good at? Different kinds of research need different team members and the relationship between them will be different, but even if it is just you and a supervisor, you need to think carefully about what you want, what you need and what you bring yourself.

Be creative and stay curious

At the end of a research project you are often left with more questions than when you started! You may have greater understanding of one aspect of the topic you were interested in, but you probably have lots more questions you want answering. Tune into this curiosity and start planning your next research study.

The best compliment I get is when someone I have worked with tells me that prior to doing the research they didn't think of themselves as a researcher, but that they have enjoyed the process, gained skills and knowledge from it, and feel like they could do research again. Professional psychologists of all kinds don't get lots of time set aside to do research, and if you are doing research it is probably due to your own curiosity and passion. The lengthy processes needed to get to the end of the research process means that this curiosity and passion can easily be squashed.

Take a moment to think back over your last research project. Where did it all start? Was there something you observed that you wanted to know more about? Is there a topic you have always been passionate about? Are you passionate about social justice and want to highlight inequalities and injustices? Or did you have to do a project in order to get qualified? Even if it is the last one, how did you choose your project – what appealed to you about it? If you think about the process, which bits did you genuinely enjoy? Was it was interviewing participants or making beautiful graphs to highlight their experience? Was it was interrogating your data to see what it really says or chatting to your friends about your exciting findings? At the end of a research project it is easy either to put research aside for a while until you have time again, or to plough straight ahead into the next project, but before you do, just take time to remember why you do this, what makes you passionate about it, and what are you curious about.

That thing you are curious about? What do you want to know about it? What is your research question? Not sure? Check out Chapter 1!

Further reading

Mertens, D. M., Cram, F., & Chilisa, B. (Eds.). (2013) *Indigenous pathways into social research: Voices of a new generation*. Abingdon: Routledge.
Smith, L. T. (2021) *Decolonizing methodologies: Research and indigenous peoples*. New York: Bloomsbury Publishing.

Wilson, S. (2008) *Research is ceremony. Indigenous research methods.* Winnipeg: Fernwood.
Books to read about who gets to create knowledge.

https://www.wiley.com/en-us/network/publishing/research-publishing/trending-stories/the-truth-behind-the-lone-genius-myth
A lovely interview about the myth of the lone genius.

Index